ROOTS AND BRANCHES

ALSO BY ROBERT DUNCAN

Bending the Bow
Fictive Certainties
Ground Work: Before the War
Ground Work II: In the Dark
The Opening of the Field
Selected Poems
Selected Proes

ABOUT ROBERT DUNCAN

Robert Duncan: Scales of the Marvelous
(Edited by Robert J. Bertholf and Ian W. Reid)

ROOTS AND BRANCHES

Poems by ROBERT DUNCAN

A NEW DIRECTIONS PAPERBOOK

First published by Charles Scribner's Sons, 1964.
First published as ND Paperbook 275, 1969.
Manufactured in the United States of America.
Published simultaneously in Canada by Penguin Books Canada Limited.
New Directions books are printed on acid-free paper.

New Directions Books are published for James Laughlin by
New Directions Publishing Corporation,
80 Eighth Avenue, New York 10011

SIXTH PRINTING

The author would like to thank the following editors for their appreciation and encouragement in printing certain of the poems in this book in the publications listed: John Wieners, *Measure*; Diane Di Prima and LeRoi Jones, *The Floating Bear*; Jack Spicer, *J*; Hugh Kenner, *The National Review*; Henry Rago, *Poetry* (Chicago); Barney Rosset and Richard Seaver, *Evergreen Review*; Bernard Waldrop, *Burning Deck*; Richard Duerden, *Foot*; Gael Turnbull, *Migrant*; Jerome Rothenberg, *Poems from The Floating World*; Robert Kelly, *Trobar*; Denise Levertov, *The Nation*; Gerrit Lansing, *Set*; Ted Weiss, *Quarterly Review of Literature*; Cid Corman, *Origin*; Stanley Persky, *Open Space*; David Schaff, *The Yale Literary Magazine*; Ron Loewinsohn and Richard Brautigan, *Change*; Donald M. Allen, *The New American Poetry 1945-60*.

CONTENTS

ROOTS AND BRANCHES (1959-60)

ROOTS AND BRANCHES

ROOTS AND BRANCHES

      Sail, Monarchs, rising and falling
orange merchants in spring's flowery markets!
messengers of March in warm currents of news floating,
      flitting into areas of aroma,
tracing out of air unseen roots and branches of sense
      I share in thought,
filaments woven and broken where the world might light
      casual certainties of me. There are

      echoes of what I am in what you perform
this morning. How you perfect my spirit!
      almost restore
an imaginary tree of the living in all its doctrines
      by fluttering about,
intent and easy as you are, the profusion of you!
awakening transports of an inner view of things.

WHAT DO I KNOW OF THE OLD LORE?

A young editor wants me to write on Kabbalah for his magazine.

What do I know of the left and the right, of the Shekinah, of the
    Metatron?
It is an old book lying on the velvet cloth, the color of olive
    under-leaf and plumstain in the velvet;

it is a romance of pain and relief from pain, a tale told of the
    Lord of the Hour of Midnight,
the changing over that is a going down into Day from the Mountain.

Ah! the seed that lies in the sweetness of the Kabbalah
is the thought of those rabbis rejoicing in their common devotions,
of the thousand threads of their threnodies, praises, wisdoms,
    shared loves and curses interwoven.

There are terrible things in the design they weave, fair and unfair
    establisht in one.
How all righteousness is founded upon Jacob's cheat upon cheat, and
    the devout
pray continually for the humiliation and defeat of Esau,
for everlasting terror and pain to eat at the nephilim.

The waves of the old jews talking
persist at the shores.

O, I know nothing of the left and the right.

The moon that moves the waters
comes clear from the earth's shadow.

All the old fears have been drawn up into the mountain that comes
    of knowing.

It is an old book of stories, the Bible is an old book of stories
—a mirror made by goblins for that Ice Queen, the Shekinah—
a likelihood of our hearts withheld from healing.

A young editor wants me to write on Kabbalah for his magazine.

Yes, for I too loved the scene of dark magic, the sorcerer's
    sending up clouds of empire and martyrdom,
the Gem made by goblins yielding its secret gold to the knowing,
enchantresses coming in to the lodestone, the star
that Adam dreams, angels

in their goblin splendors of eyes and fires
left and right ascending the ladders of letters,

El Eljon walking in the cool of His garden
—that must be all stones and gold, radioactive flowings,
molten glasses of the old volcano;

for the Kabbalah does not praise artichokes,
nor the emerald of lettuce that has a light.

What do I know of the left and the right,
who have a left hand and a right hand?
Do I put my left foot forward?

The Rabbis stop under the lemon tree
rejoicing in the cool of its leaves
which they say is the cool of the leaves of that Tree of Trees.

Look, Rabbi Eleazer says,
the Glory of the Shekinah shines from lettuces
in the Name of that Garden!

NIGHT SCENES

I

The moon's up-riding makes a line
        flowing out into lion's mane
of traffic, of speeding lights.

And in the nest of neon-glow and shadows
the nets of the city's merchants and magickers

restless move towards deserted streets where morning breaks,
holding back heaviness, emptiness, night,
      with a hand of light fingers tapping,
obscuring the drift of stars,   waiting . . .

      The whale-shark dark with the universe
pushes up a blunt nose of loneliness
      against the thin strands, shakes
the all-night glare of the street lamps,
      so that for a moment terror
touches my heart, our hearts, all hearts
      that have come in along these sexual avenues
seeking to release Eros from our mistrust.

      Our nerves respond to the police-cars cruising,
a part of the old divine threat. How in each
      time the design is still moving. The city roars
and is a lion. But it is a deep element,
      a treacherous leviathan.

The moon climbs the scale of souls.
O, to release the first music somewhere again,
      for a moment
to touch the design of the first melody!

                 2

and in what tempers restore that current
      which forth-flowing goes
a wholeness green lovers know
      as each in each a fearful happiness
sees the resolute eye in which
      opposites
spring twined forthright.

A light toward the knotted tides of dark,
into the tenderness of the crown, night's dominion,

      ::::::::: 6

I saw the Prince of Morning fall,
            opening in fucking a door of Eros.

And from the Beast a man that was Day came
shaking my heart like a storm in old trees.

        Attendant, the maiden hours dance,
        with tambourines and tiny bells clustering,
        circling to slow down ecstasy.

        Time in the folds of their skirts' motion
        sways as if from a center
                that is female
        —there being to four o'clock in the morning
                breasts, undulating belly, thighs,
                an inner temple of durations.

            The charme dissolves apace
And as the morning steales upon the night
(Melting the darkness) so their rising sences
Begin to chace the ignorant fumes that mantle
Their cleerer reason

                        sweet Ariel-song the body hears
in the mother-tides of the first magic—

Where the Bee sucks, there, the airy spirit sings, *suck I!*
Where does the bee sip? harvest what honey
        in what beehive?
In a Cowslips bell, I lie   —at the ledge

youth spurts, at the lip the flower
        lifts lifewards, at the
four o'clock in the morning, stumbling,
        into whose arms, at whose

mouth out of slumber sweetening,
    so that I know I am not I
but a spirit of the hour descending into body
    whose tongue touches
        myrrh of the morgenrot,

as in a cowslip's bell that is a moment comes Ariel
    to joy all round,
but we see one lover take his lover in his mouth,
    leaping. Swift flame of
abiding sweetness is in this flesh.

    Fatigue spreading back, a grand chorale
of who I am, who he is, where we are,
    in which a thin spire of longing
perishes,   this single up-fountain of a
    single note around which

        the throat shapes!

    3

La lampe du coeur Breton qui file et bientôt
    hoquète à l'approche des parvis
smokes, raises a music out of the light, a lamp of notes
that runs through the opening in Paradise
    into the meat from the dream the heart knows.

Flashes seize the eye's grey, forcing
    out of whose pits night's images of what day desired
    montaient vers moi
soulevées par les vapeurs d'un abîme
—figures of women passing through the strings of the harp of the sun,
    fingers that flash chains we are signals
    of protest, of assent, of longing, of anger.

O Breton, poet, we too—

where from the muscles of men working in fields see
cathedrals rise   —fume and sing out,

the early markets spreading round anthems,
the torsos of men and trucks in their own light, steaming,
by the raised lamp that surrounds the sleeping men,
circulations of food and rays!

These gates are not breasts or lions of the Queen of Byzantium,
but men working.   These grails
have men's arms and eyes, from which lamps like women fume

    at the approach of the Outer Court,
    half-naked the men mounting and dismounting,

    when I come into whose environs my heart smokes,
    la belle, la violée, la soumise, l'accablante.

She is at work in her sleep.
She draws in food from the country around her.
She compels me wandering from Breton and towards him by the plan
    of her streets.
She makes a temple of produce, in her buying and selling, a place of
    transport and litanies.
She surrounds her priests and appears in their place at the tips time
    has before falling.

Pelagius, Eckhardt, Joachim de Flore, Novalis are arms of her desire
    where she hungers for us and feeds us.

Out of André Breton
—these things translated from her savor into the savor of men's bodies
    we return to her parvis.

A SEQUENCE OF POEMS FOR H.D.'S
BIRTHDAY, September 10, 1959.

Finishd October 24, 1959.

1 *Dream Data*

The young Japanese son was in love with a servant boy.
To be in love! Dont you remember how the whole world is governd
by a fact that embraces
    everything that happens?
rendering tender and more real
     the details of the crowded dressing-room, backstage,
a closet off the hall, an office, or
    storeroom, where—furtively,
among file cabinets— but with what joy of disclosure!
    every gesture was
over-filld, more than was sensible?
     And youth in love with youth!

    Tomorrow they will be twenty years old
and being in love will go
into the aloofness the Mother in the dream counseld.

   Hold yourself above your body, she said.

The unstaind sleeves of raw silk falling from her arms flung
  dramatically above her head to show
    her defiance of —of caring?
Or was it defiance? There was
did she say? an esthetic
    stronger than sex?

And below,
the Prince in his laboratory, assisted by the boy,
    experimented in sensations, used as conductors

  ❊❊❊❊❊❊ 10

. strains and sink-stoppers he applied to the flesh of the face,
            bringing it in touch, a mechanical ground
in place of hurting.   Beyond   .

            thru an open door, they referrd to

tanks or cribs   in each which   male torsos.

            At the eve of August, Lammas tide of desire,
deformd? mutilated?   they were objects of or subjected to
preservation.   Without love,   dead in being alive,
            alive-dead.   Inhabitants of Lammas.
Bathers in hell's baths.   *These,* the Prince said

            when I was in love
            were always with me where I was.

2

            I must wake up into the morning world
            the heart is ready for, turn to ascend.
            Lift me up. Give me a hand,
            out of the hell that is still underground

            into the sunrise share, the new man.
            What Herbert in his Temple sought
            and Henry Vaughn
            upon the sunset-flooded lawn

            was suppliant for, O for Thy grace unfurld
            that love and judgment has in balance,
            all tones coming forth into one scale
            to govern and release the music of our dance.

            Thy fist unfurld, justice Thy hand,
            I seek that calls from me assent

and lays upon the questing soul Its will
in the sublime trouble of Your romance.

3

Father adopted and Father of my soul,
Father of roots and races, Father of all,
Father who is King of the dream palace,
Father attendant upon me His child,
Father who is God among the old gods,
Father seen reflected in the fathers' faces
whose love for their generations is eternal,

Father expected, Father conceald,
Father who has hidden His law in my heart,
Father who has given me keys to joy,
Father for whom the fruits of my art,
Father who has sent a message with blessing,
stand against Jehovah who is jealous in Thy place.

Father whose Love brought forth the Lover,
Father in the sun, Father in the air,
Father waiting for my return from terror,
Father who caught up Christ released from our sins,
Father who is architect of the eternal city,
help me to deliver my share of your image.

Father who grows in the plant,
Father who moves the animal,
Father whose anguish is because of our suffering,
Father whose presence means there is joy even in hell,
Father who must find His face in a mirror of me,
Father uncreated, Father evolving,
Father whose signature is in the chemical bond,
        how long you have searcht for me;

        I am your son.

The gist of the story I've known perhaps among the first stories I heard, that she died when I was born. Did they say it was in childbirth, because my head was too big, tearing my way through her agony to life? Or was it because of the fever? She died in the flu epidemic of 1919 in the aftermath of the war.

At dawn in Oakland in the cold of the year I was born, January 7th, with the sun before rising or just below the horizon in the false dawn and Saturn in his own house, in Capricorn. But that is according to the old astrological convention. Actually, the sun has advanced; the winter solstice has progresst to the sign of Sagittarius. I was born in the head of the archer.

The important thing remains: the dark of the year, the coming up into the real cold of February and March, the fever and the cold.

Edward Howard Duncan I was named. And for six months my father, the other Edward Howard Duncan, might have kept me and my two older sisters cared for me. But my father was poor, a common day-laborer. He could not afford it. Then, there must have been a period in a hospital, awaiting adoption.

The medium said: "Your mother is here."

I could only think of my adopted mother who was alive, who was not there. "What color hair has she?" I askd.

"She is fair," the voice in the medium said. "She is in the light. There, there is joyful singing. There, they are happy. She watches over you."

The voice, rarified, thrown from the head, out of place. The forced head above the green felt surface of the table. The eyes shut. Below intelligence.

"What are you, yourself?" I askd, addressing the subliminal thing. I do not remember the idiot's chatter. It was a child, eager to be calld into play. Come, old woman, you are filld with voices to say anything. My mother is alive, there, four hundred miles from here. She has dark hair and eyes.

First mother. Second mother.

Robert they calld me after a friend of my adopted father's who had died. And they kept from my old name Edward. Robert Edward Symmes.

Running across the snow towards my mother I fell, and the sun-glasses broke. That's another story that explains how I was blinded and came to be cross-eyed.

I had the double reminder always, the vertical and horizontal displacement in vision that later became separated, specialized into a near and a far sight. One image to the right and above the other. Reach out and touch. Point to the one that is really there.

But when I went to the medium, I had already taken my own name. *Robert,* for my new mother calld me Robert (Robin when she most loved me). And *Duncan* that I had from my blood father who was still alive somewhere I had heard. The other, who had been the architect, my father in the law, had died when I was sixteen.

How long my mother waited for me, all her life long, like someone waiting at last to see once more a friend or a son coming from afar before she dies. No, the second mother, waiting in doubt and in hope for me six months when I was hidden. She must have all but disbelieved that a son had been born as she had been told he would be, in the black of Saturn and the sun below the horizon or just rising

into the troubled childish day   .

O now I remember strands of hatred and love, rays of the roaring sun,
    and how I raged in my puberty reaching up into the woman you were, shaking in the throes of your mothering arms.

The medium shudderd, I think, with the change of voices. I do not remember clearly, but there were two, both childish, subnormal as they always are. Not to be trusted, cunning: "Your mother is beside you. She waves. She is very happy."

ster in our eyes, threatening to digest us and change us as you do to your own uses. With your love hunting us down to make us become carpenters like you were. We were so little you towerd above us with the threat of all overwhelming hunters. I think you didnt understand that it wasnt because we didnt know you were good. You must have thought our panic came because we didnt know you meant well.

You came along Third Street towards Market. I first heard about your coming when you were along about Howard Street. How all of us men and women fled to hide. Everywhere you were catching at us. I dont remember in the dream how it changed, how I got into another place just when you had me cornerd. I want anyway to explain how I felt.

I took Woodwork when I was in high school. It was part of our compulsory training. You see, I'm cross-eyed and I knew I couldnt work the wood right. I tried to make a breadboard for my mother for Christmas and I kept trying to plane it down so it would be level—maybe it was mixt up with making things that were at all "on the level". I know one of the lasting dismays in the task was how I had tried to cover up the poor joining of dark and light sections of wood. Sometimes when I write, sentences will be like that, labord and miserable under my hand, not fitting together in one continuous feeling, without the inner voice or sureness. —No, this wasnt high school, it was in the eighth grade. I was thirteen, and what I remember is crying and not caring what anybody thought but how miserably I ruind the work more and more with every effort to fix it up. But how can I ever tell it right? What I remember is some utter misery in me that showd up in whatever I did there, so that all could see I was not somehow a man, showd up my crying and my being afraid of what a man must do.

You see anyway, what you wanted, for me to be a carpenter, was specially wrong. You meant well, but I'd have to go deep into failure, like trying to get this letter straight, writing and rewriting.

Dont you see I'd just have to fail deeper and deeper if you caught me and made me work for you?

Isnt my own work in poetry meaningful to you? Why did you demand everywhere that we leave our vocations, put away what we were? Yet in the dream I didnt remember about being a poet. I didnt have anything to turn to. Like now, writing this letter, I see clearly that you have no regard at all for my profession of writing. And I remember—it may have been one of the materials out of which this dream in which you came was shaped—I had been talking two days before about how life becomes a trap if there is anything you cannot let go. "Well," I said then, "it's not true that I'm free to change, because I have a life-work in poetry to do." Was it that I wanted Poetry to be my Fate, and You were angry? When poetry is my fate, in the poem you are a carpenter and I am a dreamer belonging to the poem I write. That's why I'm writing a letter to you instead of a poem like DREAM DATA, because I didnt make you up, you came to me in the dream. And I wasnt a poet, I was only a frightend animal. You might have been Christ, you might have been some terrible force that would compel us to change, you might have been an angel—I try to address you as you were, for though I knew you were a carpenter, in the dream you were a hunter of men.

When I woke from the dream I thought at first about how well meant what you wanted was. I wonderd why I ran in such abject panic trying to get away from you. Carpentering was real work, it was for the good of all and without vanity. It seemd to me poetry was only an avocation and words were not needed things. The wood was real. No wonder in the dream I had nothing to turn to.

Yes, I was running away from work, from the only real work to do. And nothing would hide me.

I tried to pull the earth over me, to turn the color of nature, crouching down behind that little hummock and hoping you wouldnt find me out. Like when I was a child playing "You cant see me", when I'd just cover my own eyes with my hands and barely peek out at you through the little spaces between my fingers—or years later, that New Year's Eve in the orchard at Guerneville in the rain, when I stumbled out drunk and burrowd into the mud, letting the rain run down around me, hiding, and yet wasnt I . . . waiting to be found, fearing to be found? Yes, I think I was glad that you saw me where I was, because there was the sureness you wanted me, but you didnt understand at the same time that I was terrified.

The minute I started trying to get away from you, you saw me. The earth would not hide me, and then I tried to run for it, to climb into the deserted boxcar that was standing in the vacant lot there. Well, if I remember right, I pulld the boxcar over me to be underneath, but this part is mixt up. You had reacht Market Street by that time, and the office girls and clerks ran before you. How patiently, not to be distracted from your purpose, you bore down upon them.

The box-car may have turnd into the building where I took refuge. I thought you were surely too big to get inside the building, and, though I knew you would fish around with your hand, I was sure you wouldnt be able to look inside at the same time. I could hide somewhere out of reach.

But once I crawld into the ruind factory or warehouse, I saw the room I was in was lofty. The ceilings of the building soard into dim regions beyond my sight. This is the first time I've thought of *that*. It seemd to me that only you were outside my scale in the dream, but the shadowy great architecture about me now was *your* size, not mine. So everything in the dream was not regular size. Of course! now I remember. *That* was out of scale too—the boxcar originally had been no larger than a packing-box. I had pulld it over me and hid under it.

You were *there*. I swung up the chain that hung from the vaults above and began to be aware that I was so high up and to see that the hall was so vast—it was a giant hall—that there was room for *you* there. And you *were* there. I swung out then and hid behind the round staind-glass window at the end of the hall.

One of the most vivid things I remember was the next moment. I guess I was cowering, I know I was afraid. You could see right through the beautiful window. All the many-colord glass only brought us face to face. You lookt at me as if I were a landscape or something out beyond that staind-glass window you had been searching for, and now you had found, and you just lookt through the window at what there was to see. But, for me, I thought everything was lost. Then I had another chance! another chain! and swung free above the building and, just as I realized to my dismay that you held the other end of the chain where I went swinging as if to escape, I was loose and ran chattering along that dear branch of the tree, swinging from branch to branch with such an animal delight, if I hadnt been afraid and hadnt been back on another chain, scrambling down, a little furry animal, a monkey, to find myself croucht at the other end of the hall. Far off you stood, staring still through the window pane upon whose cross bars . . . You were now the angel who in Jess's painting, *The Casting of the Dice,* stares through the window pane where the little figure of a Jesus hangs beneath his hand lowering the frame.

I knew then that this was just the same. I knew that I was there where you were looking at me face to face. Found and yet deserted. And now, at this end of the hall where I had taken last refuge, trying to hide again under draperies, I had troubled the hall, disturbing the arrangements like I did. What good would it be?

So I'm trying to write to tell you what you were asking of me. I couldnt think then in the dream. You see you are so giant, and there is only one of you. You are all alone. There are just us little people that belong to you but we're not giants, and no matter how much you think it would be a good thing, a saving thing, if I'd become a carpenter because you imagine I would be a good carpenter like you, I'd be miserable at it, honestly I would. Cant you see? And I dont think you see our point about being afraid when you call and search us out like you do. You think of it as salvation and you cant see how it is slavery for us. You wanted me to give up everything, didnt you? and go with you, and I couldnt think about my own work in poetry I was so scared. I had nothing in the dream. I couldnt think about my home in Stinson Beach and Jess and the cats and friends coming to visit. I couldnt think about how hard it is anyway to give time to the garden and to keep things of the household in order. And these things and beings I love dont ask what you ask. You wanted me to work like you do forever and to love only as you love. You were so sure and I was so unsure. Didnt your demand strip me of what I was and ask something new? Cant you see why I ran, why I hid everywhere? What if I'd askd that of *you*? But then I couldnt imagine asking you to leave your work, because I knew that the work of the carpenter shop was real.

This morning I wonderd if I could just—well, 'by some sur-render—let you take what you need without my having to desert these unimportant things and beings that I love and that somehow seem to need me or just to share with me this helpless little happiness of the human world that now I understand, from having you come for me in that dream, is an almost pathetic homestead upon the marches of relentless power.

NEL MEZZO DEL CAMMIN DI NOSTRA VITA,

at 42, Simon Rodilla, tile-setter,
    "to do something big for America" began
the Watts towers
(this year, 1959, the officials of which city
  having initiated condemnation hearings
  against which masterpiece)

three spires
rising 104 feet, bejewelld with glass,

shells, fragments of tile, scavenged
    from the city dump, from sea-wrack,
taller than the Holy Roman Catholic church
    steeples, and, moreover,
inspired; built up from bits of beauty
    sorted out—thirty-three years of it—
the great mitred structure rising
    out of squalid suburbs where the
mind is beaten back to the traffic, ground
    down to the drugstore, the mean regular houses
straggling out of downtown sections
    of imagination defeated. "They're
taller than the Church," he told us
    proudly.

            Art, dedicated to itself!

The cathedral at Palma too
    soard above church doctrine,
with art-nouveau windows and baldachine by Gaudí
    gatherd its children
under one roof of the imagination.

            The poem . . .

"The poet,"
Charles Olson writes,
"cannot afford to traffic in any other *sign* than his one"
"his self," he says, "the man
  or woman he is" Who? Rodia
    at 81 is through work.
Whatever man or woman he is,
    he is a tower, three towers,
a trinity upraised by himself.
        "Otherwise God does rush in."

Finisht.   "There are only his own
        composed forms, and each one
the issue of the time of the moment of its creation,
not any ultimate except what he in his heat
and that instant in its solidity yield";

like the Tower of Jewels at the San Francisco
        Panama-Pacific Exposition in 1915, this
"phantom kingdom to symbolize man's
        highest aims", glittering, but

an original, accretion of disregarded
        splendors
resurrected against the rules,
having in this its personal joke; its genius
        misfitting
the expected mediocre; an ecstasy
        of broken bottles
and colord dishes thrown up against whatever
        piety, city ordinance, plans,
risking height;

                        a fairy citadel,
a fabulous construction out of
        Christianity where Morgan le Fay
carries the King to her enchanted Isle
        —all glass beads of many colors
and ricketty towers, concrete gardens,
        that imitate magnificence.

"Art," Burckhardt writes:
"the most arrogant traitor of all
    putting eyes and ears . . . in place of
        profounder worship"
"substituting figures for feelings."

The rounds contain crowns.
The increases climb by bridges.

The whole
planned to occupy life and allow
    for death:

                a skeletal remain
as glory, a raised image, sceptre,
    spectral island, most arrogant,
"to do something big for America"

    Rodia.

A DANCING CONCERNING
A FORM OF WOMEN

            Poets
            in a company
            of four
            arranged themselves for me

            feet first
            Coleridge and Creeley,
            necks and
            heads next,

            bodily Emily
            from where she'd hid
            but gladly
            dauncing,

            and a bold Lady.
            "Who are you?"

I said
"in the name of four

lines limnd
rightly
and Poetry?"
"You forgot,"

she replied and led me
backwards, "Creeley's
ma-
gic pot

and consequently that
my foot
in each verse
counts, my lament

livens the tune,
re-
arranges their feet and faces,
gives four walls to the room."

Now how good of my friend
to go
wholly
enthralld to Her

and yet to remember
cannily
while dancing
to reach round

forward to what
is behind and to find
through Coleridge's side
some likely

remembrance of me,
being there
where I werent,
and his

lifting the skirt of things this way
to show the Lady's knee and thigh
and then
recovering the Lady's thigh and knee.

"I," replied this Form of Women,
"showd him these things under
oath
and privately,

that now
he must make the most of
and needs show
to thee."

THE LAW

a series in variation
for Toby and Claire McCarroll

I

There are no
final orders. But the Law
constantly destroys the law,
erasing lightly or with turmoil
coils of the snake
evil is, referring to

imagined goods where they
radiate. What
hurts and what heals?
What hinders what intent
and what reveals?
New needs are new commands.
And this hurt good
that prescribes
the otherwise unwonted quest.

Ad-
just the law
to fit where the eye
sees what fits? or the heart
skips a beat un-
expectedly? Have these a court? Yet
hurt may a melody to the course of plain speaking give
necessary disarrangements, have been
anticipated, rememberd, thus
expected in eternity—no other
move will satisfy.

Song's fateful. Crime
fulfills the law. *Oedipus* is a
ravishing order in itself.
His tearing out his eyes—
a phrase, secretly prepared,
that satisfies.

2

To what can we conform?
They go to murder Duncan, who here
is a sleeping King.
"If it were done," the fumbling actor tells us
and just here comes into

immortal "when 'tis done,"
words "then 'twer well
it were done quickly!" Here, here,
and here,
there's such a particular law
there can be no other play,

but Shakespeare must play it out.
From the first, *in a desert place?*
or from the last, "Crownd at Scone"?

The law is everywhere we did not see
but singing
where we were fearful to sing
sang unknowingly.

3

At every stage
law abiding or breaking the law
(disobedience is not careless)
needs a code. What's the score? keys
previous to the music
not given by nature.

Justinian or Moses, whoever directs, must
propose "unnatural" restrictions
and say with a loud voice:
"Cursed be he that
    confirmeth not *all* the words of this law
    to do them"—designing therein
nets to please Satan. The Judge
must have justice as His left hand,
mercy as His right, to hold them,
if He be, Love to whom we pray is,
Fisher of Men from the cold living waters

—for the laws are nets in the seas
of men's will
that teem with such
cravings, seekings of redress, protests,
bindings upon bindings,
fates that men tie to imitate
knots that cold, hunger, hurt and disease tie;
visible defections of what is, that stir
old roots in fearful desire and throw forth
prodigies of judgment—monsters,
disastrous congregations, "acts
of God," we call them, strokes
that disable.   Yet call

upon Love too, Who by Law's naild
to a cross.   "Hail,
Christ, and make good
our loss."

4

Robin Hood in the greenwood outside
Christendom faces peril as if it were a friend.
Foremost we admire the outlaw
who has the strength of his own
lawfulness. How we loved him
in childhood and hoped to abide by his code
that took life as its law!

5

No! took an Other way as its law.
For great life itself uses us like wood
and has no laws in burning we understand,
gives no alternatives. "Is"
we think of as intransitive,

who are exchanged in being,
given over from "I" into "I",
law into law, no sooner breaking
from what we understood, than,
breaking forth, abiding,
we stand.
                    As Roethke
"breaking down, going to pieces,"
caged in a university as he is
rages as a man should
if he give over his fate to the Muses
commanding as they do
strains of a wild melody against the grain,
knots and hackings of their thread.

It's the sense of law itself demands
                    violation
within the deceitful coils of institutions.

What is
hisses like a serpent
and writhes

to shed its skin.

APPREHENSIONS

I

To open Night's eye that sleeps in what we know by Day.
        "If the Earth were animate
it should not experience pleasure when grottoes and caves are dug
    out of its back"

From which argument my mind fell away
or disclosed a falling-away,
and I saw an excavation—but a cave-in of the ground,
hiding in showing, or showing in hiding,
a glass or stone, most valuable.

According to the text

["Renaissance Cosmologies"
by Paul-Henri Michel,
Diogenes, 18]

Ficino had the idea
    life circulates from the earth
    to the stars
"in order to constitute the uninterrupted
    tissue of the whole of nature".

You've to dig and come to see what I mean.
    Eidos, Idea,
"is something to which we gain access through sight."
This defines the borderlines of the meaning.
    For what I saw was only a gleam.
    I did not bring the matter to light.

Well, I saw . . . yes, that the earth is a great toad-mother,
    a fancy figure of Tiamat,
pitted with young. But then I stood
looking down into a chain of caves most real
(that might have been washt out, gutted
 by rains from the shit-yellow clay),

an opening archaeologists or a storm had dug
(at Qumrân fragments of an old way
    stored out of sight).

Michel remarks: *"Statements of this kind*
    are all the more valuable because they are rare"
    and *"Certain concordances reveal direct and more or less*
    disguised plagiarisms."

31 ::::::::

What I saw was only a gleam.
It might have been a living thing
for it moved in the muck.
I did not search it out.
The look was enough.

(My mind had slipt again, could not
keep its place in the sentence)
"Whenever the subject is not the earth
but the universe viewd as a whole"
        "divergences appear"

And the soul was reveald where it was,
fearful, rapt, prepared to withdraw
        from knowing,
looking down into the six-foot pit where . . .

Or it was a stone that is most rare,
        moving to see,
what we call a jewel, hidden there, formd
        in pressure and the inner fire.

Ficino's text reads: *"How can one dare*
to say that this woman's womb is not living
since it produces little ones?"

2

THE DIRECTIVE

is a building. The architecture of the sentence
                allows
personal details,   portals
reverent and enchanting,

constructions from what lies at hand
                    to stand
for what rings true.

                    His concentration fixes this
                island,
a space figured in language by where is placed
                tower
and here bridge to the walls.

How they ploughd the given field in rows,
                prose and
versus . and brought landscape
                into being,

the grove interpreting and
                interpreted by the house and hearth—
                    a grave expectation

provides for the dome of many-colord glass,
                jeweld light,
carved woods and deep windows;

needs hush of the high hall that from above
is deep, a well or wall of holy spirit
                defining the humble.

                    Where there is a temple
                    man's kept from base servitude.

        Let my awe be steady
    in the rude elements of my household.
        At the window, the rose vine.

Sage Architect, you who awaken
the proportions and scales of the soul's wonder
        of stars and water,
                paeans of color
that bathe the cumulus at the horizon, yet
        direct
                discrete light
defining the lintel,

Bells tied in the foliage ring as the wind rises.

                *

        I found a monument of what I am
        around me as if waking were a dream,
        a house built in the ancient time
        when man like a salmon swam

        in currents of fire and air, in what he was,
        leapt to the ladders of desire
        and read in the stream before there were letters
        deep reflections of his cause.

        There must be a pool, dark and steady mood,
        stone and water, where this magic crossing,
        this ray of a star, catches in flow
        another time of what we always are,

        from which we start up into the live jewel,
        see joy hid where death most is,
        ready like a seed encased in its shell.
        O let the shadows and the light rays mix!

        Sage Architect of the soul and its image,
        let there be a household of these things
        where such a silence awakens our fearful touch
        and flames of beauty in old stuff rage.

I've to come into a loneliness, as if into a room
whose builder rememberd that Love stands alone
and workt in whose timbers a rude poetry
evoking the presence and weight of that crown.

The King brings his old body into its monument
in which we are rememberd, lonely and bare,
of one being, one presence,
slowly restoring the house of its kin.

The aged wood shines in the light,
surrounding and including the shine of our eyes.

*Bells tied in the foliage
ring as the wind rises!*

3

Dream or vision, the ancestors' adventure;
      new food found in famine;
or manhood in the wounds of a woman's rage;
      scooping the saintly skull
to eat of its virtue;
      theft of fire; theft of what the heart desired
made so beautiful by theft's magic that
      men still remember the walls of Troy,
the horse-traders' town; and young boys have heroic affinities,
      immune by the Mother-Dragon's blood,
except that Eros marks one spot to be betrayd as His,
      close upon Death.

All that we've lived obscured truth on these pages.

      The elemental man is a humpt bank where
         the hair grows, heapt up of time,

folded upon fold, lifted up from what he was,
      a depth of silt, into this height
         above sea level.

Compressions, oppressions—the horde gathering
      in the poorest lands,
shifting the weight of continents. And continents
      are only what giants must be.

Theosophists teach that primeval man is a vast dispersed being,
having as much intelligence in the sweep of his tail
as in his claws or those ravening jaws, back of whose
row on row of teeth ripping the meat
      a brain like a child's fist pushing those eyes;

and see the force of intellectual hunger
      focus, ravening towards such rest
a diamond has in structure, sustaind by pressure. Man
      so exclusively defined he is
         a figure of light.

         Then hunger be stem
         from what I am,
and the hero bloom as he will toward that end
      the poem imitates by admitting a form.

To survive we conquer life or must find
dream or vision, the grandfathers' fathers' trail.
      But it was my grandfather who made that trek
after the war into the Oregon Territory
and my grandmother who enterd the dragon West
      enacting what is now a map
where we crawl on hands and knees along the edge of the rug
to the house of the Bear Chiefs
      in the blood-colord light and the purple light
         from her staind-glass window cast

where by a river for a long time stayd
so that there is a continent of feeling beyond our feeling,
        a big house of the spirit,
indians and cowboys taking over the english-styled garden.
            Over and over: *"You're dead!"*
Only to jump up shouting, "This is play!"

This is play. They've come back from the wars.
            The German trophies shown on the balcony.
And the grown-ups discuss the death-throes
        of continents and civilizations.

        The tired old man
after that other war,
caught in the nets of marriage his wife wove
        taking to drink and whores
            as my grandfather did
—now that I know that story—
            but this is myth
that Freud says lies in our blood, Dragon-wise,
to darken our intelligence.

        We remember it all.
The sinister children at table reject their food,
        spewing up bits,
member by member remember, part by part
        the cast, a bit in the play,
of the eyes, of the dice, of design toward crisis.

        [reversion to First Movement]

        They had taken him out of time.
        He had taken them, parts of him,
        out of what he was, left
        detaild record of his form.

37

So that the earth
bereft of him
kept a crude resemblance.
The lowest room, at least,

stood for the head,
joind by a neck
to the trunk of the cave above.
It was not a grave then.

It was a place where a flood
had passionately dug out
his substance, leaving only his boundaries.
And it seemd a grave to me,

for I thought he was dead. No. .
it seemd a series of caves as I said.
Certainly, there were no arms or legs
clearly defined.

It did occur to me
that the hideous gleam of a crawling thing
            there at the bottom
was in the mind—
that the figure was head downwards.

            I have seen the jewel.

To open Night's eye that sleeps in what we know by Day.

            In the grievous excavation he remains,
                as if an empty place waited

                body to my soul.

::::::::: 38

Cire perdue, waste that was wax to the edge melting, forecast I've known in every touch! —thus the Lover addresst his unrest in the first uprising of the light that unspelld his surrounding dark: This night has so fingerd my soul that I awake a new, a workt figure of joy.

O play that Love makes out of Desire! What I was as a boy has run out and away so that I wept. Spectral images of manhood took shape in me.

I saw in your eyes—sudden, waiting, empty—a place I was to fill. As in the theater it can be shown, such a previousness to passion, a void
      prepared in its visible counter part—

song, *cire perdue,* river of me that flows away, melted from cast after cast, wax releasing fingerprint-fine intensions of the man from the world that is a worker in men. See! from Hesperus-Lucifer starts of light out of earliest thoughts toward me reach me, leaving scars of evening and morning,

   cire perdue of love first known,

lost wax that knew the shaping hand,

O cave of resemblances, cave of rimes!

5

(First Poem)

It is the earth turning
that lifts our shores from the dark
into the cold light of morning,
eastward turning,

and that returns us from the sun's burning
into passages of twilight and doubt,
dim reveries and gawdy effects.
The sun is the everlasting center of what we know,
a steady radiance.

The changes of light in which we dwell,
colors among colors that come and go,
are in the earth's turning.

Angels of light!   raptures of early morning!
your figures gather what they look like
out of what cells once knew of dawn,
first stages of love that in the water thrived.

So we think of sperm
as spark-fluid, many-milliond,
in light of the occult egg striking
doctrine.
            Twined angels of dark,
hornd master-reminders of from-where!
your snake- or animal-red eyes
store the fire's glare.

O flames! O reservoirs!

(Second Poem)

Handle the cards, shuffle the cards, cut and shuffle.
Distribute them once more upon the table.
Sometimes I am not permitted to read.

O I know the cards like an old poet knows his images,
but when I am not able to read they are only
numbers and faces, there are no moving pictures.

Cards of going, cards of coming . . .

These are not your cards or mine.
There is an angel of the time we are reading.
To figure his likeness men have ascribed

planetary governors, angels or gods, to the hours.
There is a god of the time where the cards fall.
You and I reading are meeting among his powers.

All things are powers within all things.
Think of the continuous presence
between the light of Venus or Mars and the eye

seeing the planet in the West in the evening
or the planet rising in the sign of Taurus near the Pleiades.
There is only one event.

There are old diagrams whose points are stars,
knots and associations that are men's gods,
or notes of a scale or possible scales to which music refers,

and think too of our speech where men
come again and again to their few words,
not of what they think they are saying

but of the thing they are telling, the mode
where they refer to the cards they are holding,
cards of going, cards of coming.

Numbers, letters, cards, words or hours
—handle and shuffle, cut and shuffle.
This one came before,

the image of grottoes or caves "dug out of the Earth's back"
arranged to suggest the cast of the Ancient of Days,
the Primordial Man.   Now it is gone.

It was in the distribution of words.

A worm or reflection of a star
moved in the depths. A star may be a crawling thing,
     as in the *old* deck,
something answers the moon or answers for the moon
     and changes movement.

Bruno of Nola saw such a universe.
    "In whatever region I am," he wrote,
"time and place are distant mountains
  changing their visages in the distant light."

(Close)

March 27th: We found after the rains a cave-in along the path near
the rosemary and thyme, disclosing the pit of an abandond cess pool.
Because of the dream fragment a month before, the event seems to
have been anticipated. A verification of the caves seen in actual life
after they had appeard in the life of the poem.

Wherever we watch, concordances appear.

From the living apprehension, the given and giving *melos,*

melodies thereof— in what scale?

Referring to these:

the orders of the sentence in reading;
the orders of what is seen in passing. There was the swarming earth;
the orders of commanding images;

the orders of passionate fictions and themes of the poet in writing;

the orders of the dead and the unborn that swarm in the floods of a man embracing his companion;

the orders of the Lord of Love. Let me await thee, Prince of the Morning;

the orders magnetic of the jewel that is secreted by the toads and coils of the brain;

the orders of the Architect building in the Likeness a temple;

the orders of the day that include the actual appearance of the pit in the garden;

the orders of stars and of words;

in these most marvelous.

> There is no life that does not rise
> melodic from scales of the marvelous.

> To which our grief refers.

SONNERIES OF THE ROSE CROSS
Erik Satie whose thought returns
TO HIS MASTER SAR PÉLADAN

*

> Everywhere the bells
> sound
> accumulating
> a steady chime
>
>   that gives

time into the depths of time.

Précieusement, he directs
the puzzled novitiate.
Does he mean
           affectedly?

           We look up to see
the silly magus administer
           with exqwisite
gestures mysterious measures

           in which

he sleeps within the hill of changing chords,

           sonorous ringings,

runes of the piano toward
Mont Ségur   reveald through rites

           as the music's lure.

           *

The eye
           whose gilt-flecks gleam in whose grey
follows
           iris-radiant purple and azure
                      emerald limnd

                      wand of the peacock-angel, one
of the many-eyed specter
           upward.

                      Précieusement!

Fakes of his glory

God evercoming into His being

shows.

*

Sar Péladan
silly old man

I have prepared for you
sequences of a cathedral in blue,

holy ghostly musical
columns and staind-glass windows.

O Magister,
because we were fond of beauty, here

a Sainte-Chapelle of the mystic rose,
an odor released in the notes changing.

Thru the obedient priest at the piano
I have prepared

instructions
for the young knight's

tapers and insurrections.

*

There must now be
too too much of beauty in this beauty.

For the spectator
there is no trial of his trust,

no contest in the ritual,
without that specter

hand infatuate of the rose
preciously, with precious care,

the rapt poseur, intent,
before the altar

of Psyche, or butterfly-wingd
Isis—some made-up

some pretend
mystery of the too divine

the Master pretends to.
Don't laugh.

Is there a place for such posing
to be containd?   for even

fakes of God to touch
some youthful trembling at the edge of God?

The Gothic has spoils in thought,
an almost girlish appearance of

solemn airs

the music takes.

NOW THE RECORD NOW RECORD

From the whole being the tree
in the green leaf goes forth,
and soon we will not see far.

The river will be obscured by the many
powers of the leaves in the light
feeding the wood. But they are nothing
lasting—conductors or translators only!

And now the spring of an urgent life
pushes up from the trunk of the idea of me,
from a whole system of ramifications,
so many mortal entrances,
seasonal stations in the visible source
that like our sun streams down,
as if it were immortal,
radiant energies of one fire.

Push forth green points of working desire, tree!
I likewise!
 Verde, verde, que te quiero verde,
whose leaves are loves and who breathes
close upon the breath of his lover
  photosyntheses of his most being,

kisses of air and light of the spring-tide.

Variations On
TWO DICTA OF WILLIAM BLAKE:

> *Mental things alone are real.*
> *The Authors are in Eternity.*

I

The Authors are in eternity.
Our eyes reflect
prospects of the whole radiance
between you and me

where we have lookd up
        each from his being.
And I am the word "each".
And you are the word "his".

        Each his being
a single glance the authors see
        as part of the poetry of what is, what
we suffer. You talkd of "freedom",
        and I saw
how foreign I am from me,

saw the spark struck from the black rock,
        saw I was not free to obey
and for a moment might have been free.

        I had only to reach up,
        restore our hands touching,
speak the words direct the authors struck.

You are the black rock, you are the spark,

        eternally.

2

How long dare I withhold myself
    my Lord withholds.

I shy a glance that he too shies.
    The authors of the look
write with our eyes
    broken phrases of their book.

    Why is it you?
Because my senses swarm,
    I fear what harm?

"Compulsion" you spoke of then
    that makes us men less than Man,
moved as we are. Move my hand,
    bright star,
if you are there, author out of the light.

    Why could I not move my hand?
    Why can I not move my hand?
waiting, a word in a moving sentence,
    just at the point where
the authors reveal (but their revelation
    is everywhere) the book.

I recognized in you my own presence
    beyond touch, within being.
What could I reach, reacht as I was?

    The authors are in eternity.

    3

I am the author of the authors
and I am here. I do not dare

rescue myself in you
or you in me. Such a dark trouble
stirs in every act.
For what do I know of from where I come?
and others shall attend me
when I am gone.

What I am is only a factor of what I am.
The authors of the author
before and after
wait for me to restore
(I had only to touch you then)
the way to the eternal
sparks of desire.

4

Come, eyes, see more than you see!
For the world within and the outer world
rejoice as one. The seminal brain
contains the lineaments of eternity.

5

Mental things alone are real.

There is no mental thing unrealized.

To be a man —but we are men
who are of one mind. For the flower of nerves
and tissue in the skull
calls, O messengers of the boundaries,
        eyes of every cell,   touch, touch,
complete me such a world as I contain

        where angels move like waves,
                convulsive energies,

lighting ways in me you do not see,
        have not seen them.

They were there for they are here.
        You overlookt or, seeing them,
changed focus and dismisst them.

        O fearful eyes,
O cells that are all doubt and reckoning,
        accommodation's slaves!

You've only to restore what I know to sight
        to realize the flash
that was eternity —a world—
        in the heart's delight.

                6

For the heart, my sister,
is likewise a dark organ, an inner
        suitor, my brother, a part
                of the whole yearning.

And there must have been a flood of,
        an up-rush, a change in pulse.
For when we see an answer,
        as the young man in moving answerd,
in leaning forward toward rapture
        where Charles Olson read,
answerd, or disturbd, some question

—the poet's voice, a whole beauty of the man Olson,
        lifting us up into   .

where the disturbance is, where the words
        awaken
sensory chains between being and being,

            inner acknowledgments
of the fiery masters —there
            like stellar bees my senses swarmd.

Here, again, I have come close upon what harm?
            where the honey is,
charmd by the consideration of his
            particular form,

as by lines in the poem charmd.

                        7

There was the event there was.

        That is

recomposed in the withholding.

The whole of time waits like a hand
        trembling upon the edge of another hand,
        trembling upon the edge of not caring,
        trembling upon the edge of its eternal answer

        That is

not ours in the withholding.

We wait, two Others, outside ever
        our eternal being

        That is

here, in this sad tableau too,
        (for us, unwilling actors)
        rapture.

The authors are in eternity

That is

in thought intensely between us,
restraint that acknowledges

the lover's kiss.

COVER IMAGES

Shaking the leaves and the blossoms
toward what red fruit
from the root in hatred, from the damnd root
that in the dark I faced again
and could not see? What kind of a man
am I? Is there such agony
hid away, crawling,
in pleasure and even joy? For surely
there is no moment that is not a cell
of eternity. Strands
of Belsen and Buchenwald
issue from Eden where
first were felt and return,
if we are children of one Man,
in us all, first-last
intention,
                transformations of rage
and cruelty

. . . seen in the dream where the Beloved
masturbated, away from me, facing
a man, partly seen, undressing or
disclosing his
nakedness in an open window . . .

a fury of sexual strands, the
inexhaustible, unsatisfied
straining, of what must be, ravening
towards unions of sight and being.

*

In the painting, the child discovers
under the clouds of wisteria and rose
(The voices in the bushes, she told me,
spoke in the leaves of these injuries,
whispers that were wisteria blooms,
blues that were bruises)   the bloody flower
hovers in an image of her mother.

The knife of what
shared ironical worker sped
in her painting the pink mother-image of the poem?
(but it was her own body)   only
the deeper flowing forth of inner color?

*

Who left the notes accusing himself
of being me? In the morning
I was relieved of what knowledge?

lifted by angels that are
rays of the actual sun
out of the solitary.

Yet these leavings, these
shreds behind day light,
of women's bodies, dismemberd lives,

renderd hideous, where they were
attackt, these hackt
remnants, partly devourd. I cannot say

clear what I so feard
and could not go back to see. These
back of furniture in deserted rooms

decaying, these too? O are these too?
returnd to the day's light?
the sun's rays?

COME, LET ME FREE MYSELF

Come, let me free myself from all that I love.
Let me free what I love from me, let it go free.
For I would obey without bound,
serve only as I serve.

Come, let me be free of this master I set over me
so that I must exact rectitude
        upon rectitude,
right over right. Today

I am on the road, by the road,
hitch-hiking. And how, from one side,
how glad I am no one has come along.
For I am at a station. I am at home
in the sun. Not waiting, but standing here.

And, on the other, I am waiting,
to be on the way, that it be *my* way.
I am impatient.

O let me be free now of *my* way, for all that I bind to me
—and I bind what I love to me,
        comforting chains and surroundings—
let these loved things go and let me go with them.
For I stand in the way, my destination stands in the way!

RISK

           that there might, may, be
a last chance.
      The last chance I had   had not
           this die's immediacy
—an old rite I had forgotten
     was a rite, cast, had feard
         and put aside

le hazard.

      It comes as an aside in a poem:
           "the cast of the dice".   Then
in H. Rider Haggard's phantasy Ayesha,
     She Who-Must-Be-Obeyd, appears
          and casts her passion (person),

her That-She-Is
     (no more than a cast of a man's phantasy)
        terrible

—not upon the scales to be weighd,
     nor is it to win all or lose—
        but she lets

not luck but the way it falls
     choose for her, lets
        the senseless arbitrate.

It throws me into the void. I could not risk
     the price of the vase —it cost too much—
        for beauty's sake.

The day's allotment
     let go —for beauty's sake?

The makers of glass
melting the glow of the fire, try us.
The traders in gold and amber try us.

They brought a blue glaze
before which our souls in the old days
withered and took flame,
Bubastis in faïence,
cat-shape out of Egypt at great cost.
Men from the North brought beads where the fire swam,
turning the mind from domestic pleasure.

Primrose, mary-gold, agapanthus,
whose flowery language is everywhere free,
grow readily in my garden.

But is there a rare herb?
come to disturb the mind towards darkness?
Solitary, priceless disclosure?

Come, say this yew grows so slowly
its height is ancient, its beauty
reaches into the heart of me.

Grave Yew, what assents?
as if it too
had root and took green
at hell gate?
drew down the sun's light
into its shade?

The sky on certain days has such a blue
that means no comfort, that intensifies.

This "sky-is-the-limit" reach
now acclaim! I had not the means to buy the vase
means what surrender? The lure

Loki or Mercury contrives must be
workt by the dumb smith in whose honest
craft guile melts to form what we longd for.

We cannot divide the costly luster,
the lovely sheen, from the sound art
—quick silver, fool's gold,
the mirror flash or the turquoise glaze.

It's not Beauty it must reach, but
towards Beauty it must reach
unsatisfied.

The incorporate dissatisfaction!
And that it be rare! beyond our means!
to bring life to the risk.

*

This anyway (a hunch)
for the way they play the cards. Wealth!

There are just the cards of each hand.
Riding, not what they know, but the risk
for the play of the game, with high stakes.

Ayesha holds her self
as if-she held a challenged card.
I will draw my self out of the chance.

No, it was not like this.
I am troubled.   I do not dare
go as the cards, dice, painted sticks go.
I playd safe and did not

buy the vase.

Outward the caravans go,
      cut loose. The image *does*,
will *not* do. Lose sense toward what we do not know?

    They cast the dice at every point.
        ⚃ four,
and the heart dreams of the lost numbers.
       ⚄ five, and the heart
          dreams of the lost numbers.

He, who ready to be poor, a millionaire!
    that there might be, everlasting
        chance, obedience,
that close!

       Risk
    for sake of the lure, that there might be
      this die's immediacy,

an old rite I had shunnd.

    *

The millionaires at marble tables

in sight of the yew trees

    throw their lives upon the numbers.

FOUR SONGS THE NIGHT NURSE SANG

I

    How lovely all that glitters
    gold!

"Day unto day uttereth speech,
and night unto night
sheweth knowledge"

As in the old story
at the shores of the sea
the white swan is a maiden
and sheds her clothes,

the Moon sheds her light and returns.
With her white story
the wave breaks. See!

This I lost I have found in you.
Now I have seen fate with new eyes.

O Swan, the lover has taken away
your covering cast at the wave's edge.

Dance on! Your arms
embrace shadows, and you fling them out

into the sands, the years round you.
Your wings that were youth are gone!

The moon bathes nude in the cloud foam.
The black waters rush
into the light places.

2

It must be that hard to believe, for belief
must resist belief, pine-cone
that waits for death's fire to release its seed,
    —the Beast betrayd, forgotten,

at the edge of the pool dying, love withheld—
for the fire that destroys the living tree.

The Beast is the lord of the heart's need.
He must be hideous.
His is the Rose.
He is the First One.
Ask the Sun. Ask the Moon.
Go with the winds to the world's end.
He is beyond.

> *Come, my bride,*
> *Love has such need, He dies!*

The father's claim is what he fears. He warns her,
Do not return. He gives her
magic mirror, ring and glove
in trust. He tests her! *Tell no one*
your good fortune. Be on guard.
> *My love is here.*

It must be that hard to believe!
She must leave.

> *I have only a beast's heart,*
> *But O, return!*

Something must be lost, stolen.
Something must be told that should have been kept,
known by heart. He is all but forsworn.
Home could have won.

But the fate's turnd in the loss.
What was lockt
's released. O

most dear! the Beloved cries,
whose heart strains to answer the Beast's
enquiring eyes—   *Love I am here!*

> *Thou hast left the beast in need.*
> *At death's pool I lie.*
> *Now is the time to cry out*
> *against the human tree.*

> "Seeing and hearing all things
>   the eyes and ears of the great King waiting"
> *I have been waiting to hear,*
> *I have been waiting to see,*

seed in the burnt ground, past belief,
messenger come with news too late,
past the hour, past the bound,

            your voice that cries
Most dear!
            your searching eyes.

3

Madrone Tree that was my mother,
Cast me a cloak as red as your flower.
   My sisters don't know me,
   My father looks for me,
And I am by name the wind's brother.

Madrone Tree, from your thirsty root
feed my soul as if it were your fruit.
   Spread me a table and make it fair.
   Cast down splendor out of the air.
My story has only the wind's truth.

Madrone Tree, red as blood,
that once my mother was, be my rod.
    Death came when I was born.
    And from that earth now you are grown.
My father's a shadow, the wind is my god.

    4

Let sleep take her, let sleep take her, let sleep
           take her away!
The cold tears of her father
have made a hill of ice.
        Let sleep take her.

Her mother's fear has made a feyrie.
        Let sleep take her.
Now all of the kingdom lies down to die.
        Let sleep take her.

Let dawn wake her, if dawn can find her.
    Let the prince of day take her
from sleep's dominion at the touch of his finger,
    if he can touch her.

The weather will hide her, the spider will bind her

    : so the wind sang.

O, there she lay
in an egg hanging from an invisible thread
spinning out I cannot tell whether

from a grave or a bed, from a grave or a bed.

STRUCTURE OF RIME XV

O mask of the mandrill!
knuckle-dancing night-prowler! from your
hut among the everlastings you come,
animal figure no older than we are,
     and mimic my own, ready-made, mind mandrill,

having a name   who gave you?

                         Call back
into my heart that raging woman
outcast.   Thou art the first of our play then!
     Cast out   the lashes of your eye   over us!

I'll be a tear, swim to the brim,
dew the Sun casts down   to the rose of dawn.

How the lioness in the maiden smiles!
The too-full cup trembles in the hand and
Day spills.   The mandrill roars.
Eyes in his fiery mask, magenta and blue-striped face.

The lioness made demure from cruelty
          casts down her eyes
                    before our frightend eyes.

The sun is at noon.

She leaves nor tracks nor shade.

The maskt figure dances
where the eye looks.

STRUCTURE OF RIME XVI

Back to the figure
of the man in the drill dancing.

His form enters the animal form. His stiff prick bears its head
to the music. The makers of images scribble dancing limb upon
dancing limb, phrase after phrase, horned head within horned head.

The voice dreaming within the bear skull said:

> *The bees have left the hives of my dream.*
> *The sun has not died, but in the rose of night and day*
> *the winged denizens of the light are gone,*
> *no longer to the seminal tip come,*
> *no longer to my naked bone.*
>
> *The honey is burnd into the rock.*
> *This I have seen where I went out.*
> *The bees have left the animal hive*
> *nor in the starry lanterns swarm.*

O my soul,
now man's desolation
into his beginnings return!

STRUCTURE OF RIME XVII

This potion is love's portion. This herb
her bliss.

Helen among the wraiths
offerd this cup. Life's light in her eyes

lit the lioness wrath.
In every part this mask is worn.

Climbing toward Its place in the sentence, the Word
    toward the sublime heard
Kundry laugh or came upon the edges
    of such a witch's smile.

He drank love from the maiden's lips.

    There is nor crown nor cross   .

                that does not reflect the serpent's scale
catching the sun's rays, the many faces   .

                  mirrord, the power and froth of the
sea's depths and shallows,
        the masst glare.

This potion is love's portion. The heart of tomorrow's rose is today's
sorrow for tomorrow is gone. Yesterday has come into the song that
Helen in the sunlight sings:

> *This moment in my heart is crowded,*
> *masst with the glare of many kings.*
> *This hour is restless, masst with dead faces.*
> *This place falls away from its time.*
> *This rose falls away from its core.*
> *This cup falls away from my lover's hand and he shuts*
>   *his eyes.*

> *This herb is thistle, everlasting.*

Desire paces Eternity as if it had bounds, craving death.
The Word climbs upward into Its crown.

    Now for this time the lovers lie
    where Helen among the wraiths
    wreaths her spell.   Of thistles made.   *This herb*
        her bliss.

STRUCTURE OF RIME XVIII

Kundry was Wagner's creation. And they brought Tefnut back, from her wilderness, into their company, brought the wilderness into the heart of Egypt, drinking and dancing before her in masks of the dog and the mandrill. Have you not seen the Muse's face? her tawny eyes, her lips curld back from her flashing teeth? Have you not held Kundry's laugh at bay? Knowest thou pathos, the poet's art before time's abyss?

Wagner's head floating where ours was, flukes of chords going out from passion into leitmotif, gatherings of fervent listeners in the place where I was. To be at the end of things. To be in the beginning. Evening's *rot*. The morning's red. The red flowing out into the orchestral twilight. Passionate twinklings in women's hair.

At mid-century the bells ring where we are the numbers are. The years go on as once before. The seasonal heroes, the changing stanzas, the unfolding melodies, the fashioning of eternities.

Now, in the wind, sparrows ride the tossing branches of the pyracanthus. The burnd sea smokes into spray in the slanting light. Upward the birds from the bronze berries go.

Let this time have its canto.

OSIRIS AND SET

members of one Life Boat are
that rides against Chaos,
or into the night goes, driving back
those darknesses within the dark,
as Harry Jacobus saw them on our mountain,
trolls of the underground.

Set lords it over them,
dark mind that drives before the dawn rays.
              He is primitive terror, he is the prow,
he is first knowing
and, striving there, at the edge,
              has all of evil about him.

              Yes, he fought against Osiris,
conspired, scatterd the first light.
              He seduced the boy Horus, hawk-ghost of the sun,
to play the Hand to his cock.
He comes into the court of the law to remind us.
              He gives us the lie.

At one time our mother's brother, Set, was "Father"
        and taught us —what? ruining
our innocence. The great boat of the gods
        penetrates the thick meat,
sending quick nerves out that are tongues of light
        at the boundaries.   Foot, hand,
lips: a graph in *Scientific American,* September 1960,
        shows the design of sensory and motor intelligences.
We are so much mouth, mask, and hand,
        the hidden plan of volition can be read
              (a secret that is presented to be seen
remaining secret) in the closed palm,
              in the human face.

              The radiant jewel of our own sun
held aloft by the dung beetle is the Child,
        our About-To-Be, Presence
in what's present.   There is nothing else.

              Feeling and motion, impression and expression,
                    contend. Drama
              is the shape of us. We are

ourselves tears and gestures of Isis
as she searches for what we are ourselves,

Osiris-Kadmon into many men shatterd,
        torn by passion.   She-That-Is,
our Mother, revives ever   His legend.
        She remembers.   She puts it all together.
So that, in rapture, there is no longer
        the sensory-motor homunculus
subduing the forces of nature, Horus contending with Set,

        but the sistrum

        sounds through us.

    The Will wherein the gods ride

        goes forward.

*

        Hail! forgotten and witherd souls!

Our Mother comes with us   to gather her children!

    Now it is time for Hell
to nurse at the teats of Heaven.

        Dark sucks at the white milk.
    Stars flow out into the deserted souls.

In our dreams we are drawn towards day once more.

WINDINGS

TWO PRESENTATIONS

I

[*After my mother's death in December 1960, there were two returns of her presence in February and March of 1961. The first came in a dream.*]

"*We send you word of the Mother.*"
Was it my mother? our mother?
In the dream it was a blessing or a key
she brought, a message.
Was it H.D.'s frail script?

It was she, I thought, but the sign
was of another. It was a help
(for my mind is in great trouble)
to receive the letter.

But I was cold, lying in the narrow bed,
naked. When did I lie there so?
    The first light of morning
came in over me, a cold thin wave
where nerves shrank back from the bruise.

Who gave me the note? Only I
accuse myself of lying here in the cold,
shaking in the drafts of light,
hugging to the scant cover.

For I have lost heart,
my mind is divided.

[AFTERTHOUGHTS: *November 1961. Working on the H.D. Book, I had begun to fear her death as a forfeit or foundation of the work.*

My first mother in whom I took my first nature, the formal imperative of my physical body and signature, died when I was born. I was motherless then, "in the cold", for six months before my second mother found and adopted me. But the "When did I lie there so?" seems to refer to some cold back of this period of loss, as, in turn, "the Mother" is back of my mothers.

When I was born, what gave birth to me fell back dead or died in the labor towards my success. Was she alive or dead when I drew my first "breath" and utterd, threw out, my first cry? In taking heart, another heart was lost. What blessing, what key then?]

2

[*In the change from my birth name, Edward Howard Duncan, to my name by adoption, Robert Edward Symmes, the hidden or lost name is Howard.*

The second presentation came while I was riding the Union-Howard busline from the Marina to North Beach. I had begun a poem addresst to my mother, when the hysterical talk of a school-girl broke in, dictating fragments of a message that seemd meant for me and at the same time to direct the poem.]

You are gone and I send
as I used to
    with the salutation *Dear Mother*

the beginning of a letter
     as if it could reach you.

Yet *Dear Mother* could catch at my heart to say
     —and did when I was a child, as you
are now a child among shades—
     as if the words betrayd
a painful nearness and separation.

"It's this poem I wrote and I calld it *My Soul!*"
Was she talking to me? Her voice carries
above the din of high-school girls chattering,
 crowding the bus with shrill bird voices.

"It's this poem I wrote, see!"

She waits, and when I look up from where I am writing . . .
Did she see me writing here? How did I hear
     her voice if not directed in the crowd to me?
Laughing, the fat little Hindu girl
turns her eyes from my glance, triumphant.

"I write so many, see, all the time.
  And this one I lost. That's why I say
  I lost *My Soul.*"

Does she say anything that comes into her head
to hold my attention?
"Well, you didnt go over and pull me out,"
she shouts to some girl I can't see.

"I had such a cramp in my leg
  and I almost drownd.
  I thought I was all alone."

Like *that* then. Her voice, too,
came thru to me,

swimming in the flood of voices as if alone,
catching my attention
—a sheaf of poems hysterical girls
might carry about, carry-on about,
their souls or names . . .
loves? "You'll never love anyone," you said, Mother,
so long ago.

*

          Caught in the swirl of waters,
bobbing heads of the young girls, pubescent,
    descending from the bus,
pass on or out, into the street beyond
    —one dark Hindu face among them passes
    out of my ken.

Are you out there alone then like that?
Or did your own mother come, close in,
 to meet you. As your sister, looking forward or back
from her eighty years, said,
"Mother will be there when I die,
waiting for me." Her throat
catching at the evocation.

    But, of that other Great Mother
or metre, of the matter . . .

My letter always went alone
    to where
I never knew you reading.

AFTER A PASSAGE IN BAUDELAIRE

Ship, leaving or arriving, of my lover,
my soul, leaving or coming into this harbor,
among your lights and shadows   shelterd,
at home in your bulk, the cunning
regularity and symmetry thruout
of love's design, of will, of your
attractive cells and chambers   .

riding forward, darkest of shades
over the shadowd waters   .
into the light, neat, symmetrically
arranged above your watery reflections
disturbing your own image, moving as you are

. What passenger, what sailor,
looks out into the swirling currents round you
as if into those depths into a mirror?

What lights in what port-holes
raise in my mind again   hunger and impatience?
to make my bed down again, there, beyond me,
as if this room too, my bedroom, my lamp at my side,
were among those lights sailing out
                    away from me.

We too, among the others, passengers
in that *charme infini et mystérieux,*
in that suitable symmetry, that precision
everywhere, the shining fittings, the fit
of lights and polisht surfaces to the dark,
to the flickering shadows of them,
we too, unfaithful to me, sailing away,
leaving me.

L'idée poétique, the idea of a poetry,
that rises from the movement, from the
outswirling curves and imaginary figures
round this ship, this fate, this sure thing,

est l'hypothèse d'une être vaste, immense,

compliqué, mais eurythmique.

Shelley's ARETHUSA set to new measures

1

Now Arethusa from her snow couches arises,
Hi! from her Acroceraunian heights springs,
down leaping, from cloud and crag
jagged shepherds her bright fountains.
She bounds from rock-face to rock-face streaming
her uncombd rainbows of hair round her.
    Green paves her way-fare.
    Where she goes there
    dark ravine serves her
    downward towards the West-gleam.
As if still asleep she goes, glides or
    lingers in deep pools.

2

    Now bold Alpheus
aroused from his cold glacier
strikes the mountains and opens
a chasm in the rock so that
all Erymanthus shakes, and the black
south wind is unseald,

from urns of silent snow comes. Earthquake
    rends asunder
thunderous the bars of the springs below.

    Beard and hair of the River-god
      show through the torrent's sweep
where he follows the fleeting light of the nymph
      to the brink of the Dorian,
      margins of deep Ocean.

3

    Oh save me! Take me untoucht, she cries.
    Hide me,
for Alpheus already grasps at my hair!
    The loud Ocean heard,
to its blue depth stirrd and divided,
taking her into the roar of its surf.
    And under the water she flees,
    white Arethusa,
the sunlight still virginal in her courses,
    Earth's daughter, descends,
billowing, unblended in the Dorian
    brackish waters.

        Where Alpheus,
    close upon her, in gloom,
    staining the salt dark tides comes,
black clouds overtaking the white
    in an emerald sky, Alpheus
eagle-eyed down streams of the wind pursues
    dove-wingd Arethusa.

4

    Under those bowers they go
    where the ocean powers

brood on their thrones. Thru these coral woods,
    shades in the weltering flood,
    maiden and raging
    Alpheus swirl.

Over forgotten heap, stone upon stone,
    thru dim beams
    which amid streams
weave a network of colord lights they go,
    girl-stream and man-river after her.

    Pearl amid shadows
    of the deep caves
that are green as the forest's night,
    swift they fly,
with the shark and the swordfish pass into the wave
    —he overtaking her,
    as if wedding, surrounding her,
spray rifts in clefts of the shore cliffs rising.

    Alpheus,
          Arethusa,
               come home.

5

When now from Enna's mountains they spring,
    afresh in her innocence
Arethusa to Alpheus gladly comes.
Into one morning two hearts awake,
at sunrise leap from sleep's caves to return
    to the vale where they meet,
drawn by yearning from night into day.

Down into the noontide flow,
    into the full of life winding again, they find
their way thru the woods

and the meadows of asphodel below.
Wedded, one deep current leading,
        they follow to dream
in the rocking deep at the Ortygian shore.

        Spirits drawn upward,
        they are divided
into the azure from which the rain falls,
        life from life,
seeking their way to love once more.

AFTER READING H.D.'S
HERMETIC DEFINITIONS

I

What time of day is it?
What day of the month?
H.D. read *quatrième* for *quantième*
in Perse. Today

the sky is overcast—dove's
(that may be her *nun's*) grey—
the light diffuse.

The light's everywhere diffused,
yet
we must take our direction
from the sun's quarter,

as if accurately, obey.
I cant remember, are the bees confused?
(I cant find the bee book
—the way books can get out of hand!)

They fly
by polarized light, take their way
in dance
making their map

as we likewise in song
keep time, but ("If you lose something,
you look *everywhere*—"
He is angry because I disturbd lunch

asking, Where is the bee book?
and could not figure out
—Would they lose their way,
the sun-track

under cloud-ceiling of grey,
the *quatrième*, as we might
lose the day of the month,
as if in song its key, not

know what moon in what season.

2

I do not remember
bees working over the garden on such a day.
But in the full sunlight
the warmth of its fire

hums;
and, coverd with pollens,
the honey gatherers
go to the heart of things,

shaking and waking the flowery horns,

taking the sweet of song
to fill their dark combs.

3

In the poem there is
"—*Are you dead in the darkness?*"
Who sleeps in the hive
where the Queen's honey is mixt?

Which they prepare
by what we call *instinct,*
as if they were sure,
nursing their own

Isis—"*générateur, générant*" the poem calls her
—drones and that other
Dreamer or Mother of them all
"who orderd, ordaind or controlld this"

the goddess or nurse commands
"*Write, write or die*".
We too write instinctively, like bees,
serve the Life of the Hive,

coverd with pollens out of time,
gold of the hour, tumble,
fly under maps of the sun's measure
on wings (words) that are winds

(melodies)
in the song's light
    stored
in the Queen's ward.

4

But the truth, he told me, was
he wasnt angry about lunch.
It was because
I hid what I wanted

from myself, made
the ease of the thing impossible;
teaching the mind
not to find the sun's rime;

setting the whole house into an uproar
—Is it *one?* Is it *tone?* Is it
imagination? What word are you
looking for?

(In a mimeographt "Lesson", of Dr. Quimby
  On the Subconscious, I find
  "He also calls it 'the book'
  and he said

We are not any wiser than the book we have written")
where the bees came in,
came to mind, from *their* place or time
into this place, misplaced,

when I rememberd not where the book was
but their song in the sun.

STRAINS OF SIGHT

I

He brought a light so she could see
Adam move nakedly in the lighted room.
It was a window in the tree.
It was a shelter where there was none.

She saw his naked back and thigh
and heard the notes of a melody

where Adam out of his nature came
into four walls, roof and floor.

He turnd on the light and turnd back,
moving with grace to catch her eye.
She saw his naked loneliness.

Now I shall never rest, she sighd,
until he strips his heart for me.
The body flashes such thoughts of death
so that time leaps up, and a man's hand

seen naked catches upon my breath
the risk we took in Paradise.
The serpent thought before the tomb
laid naked, naked, naked before the eyes,

reflects upon itself in a bare room.

2

In the questioning phrase the voice
—he raises his eyes from the page—
follows towards some last
curve of the air, suspended above

its sign, that point, that   .
And asks, Who am I then?
Where am I going? There is no time
like now that is not like now.

Who?   turns upon some body where
the hand striving to tune
curves of the first lute whose strings are nerves
sees in the touch the phrase will

rise   .   break
as the voice does? above some moving obscurity

ripples out in the disturbd pool,
shadows and showings where we would read
—raising his eyes from the body's lure—

what the question is,
where the heart reflects.

DOVES

[On June 8, 1961, news came that H.D. had had a stroke. In July
Norman Pearson wrote: "The part of the brain which controls
speech has been injured, so that she cannot recall appropriate words
at will. Yet she does have fiercely the desire to communicate, and
strikes her breast in passionate frustration when there is no word
at her tongue's tip. Sometimes whole sentences will come; some-
times, everything but the key word. So it is 'I want . . .' but one
can never tell what it is she wants."]

I

Mother of mouthings,
the grey doves in your many branches
code and decode what warnings
we call recall of love's watery tones?

    hurrrrrr
    harrrrrr
    hurrr   .

She raises the bedroom window
to let in the air and pearl-grey
    light of morning
where the first world stript of its names extends,

where initial things go,
beckoning dove-sounds recur
     taking what we know of them

from the soul leaps to the tongue's tip
     as if to tell
               what secret
in the word for it.

          2

The birds claws scraping the ledges.
I hear the rustling of wings. Is it evening?
The woodwinds chortling or piping,
sounds settling down in the dark pit where the orchestra lights glow
as the curtain rises, and in the living room,
at another stage,
lamps are lit.

          3

     The lady in the shade of the boughs
     held a dove in her two hands,
     let it fly up from the bowl she made
     as if a word had left her lips.

     Now that the song has flown
     the tree shakes, rustling in the wind,
     with no stars of its own,
     for all the nets of words are gone.

     The lady holds nothing in her two hands
     cupt. The catches of the years are torn.
     And the wood-light floods and overflows
     the bowl she holds like a question.

     Voices of children from playgrounds come
     sounding on the wind without names.

We cannot tell who they are there
we once were too under what star?

Before words, after words   .   hands
lifted as a bowl for water, alms or prayer.
For what we heard was no more than a dove's

    hurrrrrr
    harrrrrr
    hurrr

        where the Day slept
after noon, in the light's blur and shade
the Queen of the Tree's Talking
hears only the leaf sound,
whirrr of wings in the boughs,

the voices in the wind verging into leaf sound.

    4

I wanted to say something,
that my heart had such a burden,
or needed a burden in order to say something.

Take what mask to find words
and as an old man come forward
into a speech he had long waited for,

had on the tip of his tongue,
from which now   .   O fateful thread!
Sentence that thru my song most moved!

Now from your courses the flame has fled
making but words of what I loved.

RETURNING TO THE RHETORIC
OF AN EARLY MODE

If I think of my element, it is not of fire,
of ember and ash, but of earth,
nor of man's travail and burden
to work in the dirt, but of the abundance,
the verdant rhetorical. Servant of the green,
the Gardener of the Hesperides returns,
sometime no more than pompos of the poem,
a claim I made on some modal prince
I thought I had seen so real he was mine
received in the music-magic of Sitwell or of Stevens,
robed round in sound, rich as a tree
in full foliage of metaphor, flower and fruit.

What actual gardener turning the dark earth
comes now in a cloud of verbiage
over the adoring ground, a continual elegy,
as if man's falling away were only
a falling of leaves to the rich loam,
came in my twenties a figure of green panic?
a storm in the branches of what I was, shaking
till all the rising music fell thru its melodies
to rest in the bed of an abiding earth,
in the still riming return to its first rhetoric.

There were actual orchards. There were actual men.
I knew the actual ache of my arms reaching
in the work of pruning, thinning the crop,
        picking the ripe fruit,
was empty—for these were not the trees,
this was not the ground, the primordial
        dirt and seed
where the form of my tree slept.

Grief was of the ground.
Grief was of the seed.

I found the form of a man in his redundance,
sun-dancer, many-brancht in repeating,
many-rooted in one thing, actual only
in time so fleet the real trembled
undoing itself. Who was in truth I knew
sublime messenger or message in himself,
geist of rhapsodic excess in a time
despising the rush, the being carried away?
This divine image coming forth in his name
of a need so intense it gatherd up joy
like the long trunk of an other self
turning on his thighs to open life's arms.

Self was of the ground.
Self was of the seed.

The angel was of the gesture, appeard as the lure of flesh,
muscular invested, a pure emblematic physique,
standing for what scripture? Who are you?
where again you go as ever
attendant and guardian of all verdant thought.

"I was led down the garden path", I was carried away.
I was led in the way. I was led on
by a wraith whose time was of green afternoon the wish,
by a rhetoric, all the sweet sap
of the trees singing, sweet and bitter in the one vein.

My yearning was of the ground.
My yearning was of the seed.

Hidden wherein
the workings of ecstatic form.

TWO ENTERTAINMENTS

*

another one for Helen Adam

THE BALLAD OF
THE FORFAR WITCHES' SING

out of the Scots into our American tongue

> "*Andrew Watson hade his usuall staff in his hand, altho he be a blind man yet he danced alse nimblie as any of the companye, and made also great miriement by singing his old ballads, and that Isobel Shyrrie did sing her song called* Tinkletum Tankletum, *and that the divill kist every one of the women*" —testimony at the trial of the Forfar Witches.

Sing your song, Shyrrie, and you'll get a cold kiss.
For Tinkletum Tankletum gives a twist to the moon
that shines on my eyeballs as if I could see.
I know, I know, I'll be dancing soon.
When I hear your old voice fly up to its tune,
that music raises dancers out of the mist.

For my blind eyes lie in my head
like stones that would stare lassie or lad
out of their stride, and my heart's a nest
where a mangy cat that was once sweet yearning
nurses wild kittens at her burning tits,
and the moon stirs my feet along with the rest.

Sing Tinkletum Tankletum, Isobel Shyrrie.
I feel such a merriment raised to your beat
the white stones must be dancing in the moon's heat,

and the Forfar bones from the graveyard ground
will be calling me up to join the round.
For the toes of my feet twitch to your numbers
and I'll soon be dancing in what I can't see!

    :and that Isobel Shyrrie did sing her song
    :and that the divill kist all and one

But see! my staff twitches and turns in my hand
with a witch-hazel's wisdom to find out tears.
Raise up your voices and dance the Diane,
tomorrow the Christians will be at our doors.
They're gathering wood to feed a good fire.
They'll be hunting the Hare, they'll be hunting the Wren.
Sing your song, Shyrrie, for we've too many years,
with the cold of the moon aglint in our eyes
and the cold on our lips that the townsman fears.

O take the shaking of my hand in your hand
and we'll be done in the dance that mocks the bird.
For our Master's the Man with the Cold Claw
who flies with the nightjar out of time's maw
with a song in old hearts that sours the word.
Sing Tinkletum Tankletum, Isobel Shyrrie,
as first I ever that gay song heard.

They're calling the jury, they're setting their snares.
The hounds of the law are baying again
to hunt the cat-foxes out of their lairs.

Sing your song, Shyrrie, and raise it high
till a glare of the old wildness comes into my eye
and the dead begin hopping like toads from the stones,
croaking and moaning "To die! to die!"
Such kisses and fumblings there be in old bones!

:and that Isobel Shyrrie did sing her song
:and that the divill kist all and one.

Give us Tinkletum Tankletum before we go,
and let's us and the dead make merry once more.
I can hear at time's door the first cock's crow.

  —Do you know the Wren,
  the cow's own mother?
  or the toad who gives milk
  to nurse the Sun's brother?
  Sing Tinkletum Tankletum sops-in-wine.
  Under the hill there lives a fine lady.
  The Moon's got one eye
  and she's got the other.
  Sing Tinkletum Tankletum my hump's a great bother!

They'll be at the door before I wake,
so sing it once more, Isobel Shyrrie.
For they're beating my soul from its sleepy brake.
Sing your tinkle of elvesbells under my feet,
your tankle of fernscrowns over my head,
your Tinkletum Tankletum, Isobel Shyrrie,
for they're out with their witch-hounds
  and they've enterd the house.
They're shaking me up from my sweet bed!

They've found out my lizard. They'll find out my mouse.
What shall I do then? Sing Tinkletum Tankletum

  —Singing sops-in-wine
  I'll give you a sign
  a strawberry mark beneath your wing
  to make you a bird and teach you to fly
  before it's too late,

Tinkletum Tankletum,
and a toad bye-and-bye
a carrion baby baked in a pie
who will crouch in your plate and then
leap to your eye and learn you to sing
Tankletum Tinkletum when the fire burns high!

Hell runs to my fear where the town bells ring,
and the sorrow in my soul is like a well gone dry.
I'm only Old Watson, Blind Andy, Old Croaker!
tho I've danced with the best beneath the dark sky.
The Black wool's on the one side
and the white wool's on the other.
The worm sings merrily in the ripe corn.
And I cry to my neighbors "Have pity on the Old One!
Love's left me markt like the devil's brother!

"O let me alone, for I was a lame dancer,
a joker over the grave stones—yes, but a blind one."
Now white's the night and black's the day.
The live are to burn us, with the dead we'll away.

**

A COUNTRY WIFE'S SONG

from *A Play with Masques*

Now if you doubt my story
you'll never find me out.
I'll gather wool from the gallow's tree
and knit my bridal shroud.

When I was but a young girl,
   my mother said to me
Ye think ye'll marry yon bonny carl
   and ye will faithful be.

But the moon will change
   and so will you.
I'll teach you a devil's trick or two
   a simple charm
   twill do no harm,

For a wife can lie by her husband's side
and dance besides where the green men pipe
   and ancient crones
   with their lusty drones
       betray the Honeymoon.

When I was still a willing wife
   Old Gowdie said to me
Ye'r all this day for the married life
   and ye would faithful be.
But the human heart will run about
   and is faithless as the sea.

I'll teach you a woman's way to sew
   a fancy trick
   with stone and stick
when ye'll know not whither to stay or go,

For a wife can lie by her husband's side
and dance besides where the green men pipe
   and souls are lost
   at double crosst
       beneath the Honey Moon.

   Now if you doubt my story
   I'll change my tune for you.

I'd ravel the shroud in a thorn tree
and let the ends hang loose.

When I was first an adulteress
    my lover said to me
When you were born you were one of us
    and I have set you free.

For few are those that God once chose
    when first the human lot He cast.
The rest are pickings for the crows
    and base iniquity.

I'll teach you a faithless ruse to try
when lust hides out in your sleepless eye,
    a puppet face
    to take your place,

For a wife can lie at her husband's side
and dance besides where the green men pipe
    for the fairy feast
    and fucking the beast
            behind the Honey Moon.

And now that I've lived forty years
    my mother spoke most true.
My eyes have used up all their tears.
I've known the cold the whole world fears,
    and I have much to rue.

But I've learnd to play the fickle moon
and leave my traces where I'd come,
    to pray my pay—
    ter noster back,
First the white and then the black.
The time is late and the hour comes soon.

For a wife can lie at her husband's side
and dance besides where the green men pipe,

          leaping there
      in the shape of a hare,
            betimes the Honeymoon.

WHAT HAPPENED : PRELUDE

ARGUMENT. As two sisters work in the composition of a musical play, one of them acts as Poet and is inspired by certain angels of the Muse who appear in the work as Puss-in-Boots and Anubis—"little curtains open to reveal two life-sized automatons, mechanical marvels of the period." The Muse then may be Isis, and the body of the work seen in this dimension is the Osiris, where Bubastis and Anubis attend from the first the putting together of the play. These higher orders have their own music, so that the Poet receives the word thru-out, songs and recitative, along the lines of insistent and reoccurring tunes. These themes we recognize as the circulations or rounds of Osiris.

This is the stage where forces of the old mysteries work to trans-form into meaning again the hackneyd traditions of popular entertainments, to enact the supernatural. The Poet creates the Worm Queen, impersonating the Underworld, and evokes every-where images of burning and darkness—"A Ballad Melodrama." Susan, the ingénue of the play, engaged by her false or step aunt to the vain Neil Narcissus, does not belong to their world but, sleep-walking, belongs to the orders of dream and longing, where in the shadows she meets her true love, a dead sailor. All the forces of the Worm Queen—murder, fire and earthquake—announced by her automatons, move to rescue Susan from the trivial and to unite her in the troth that poetry keeps with the grave.

The play is twice presented in its authentic form by the Poet, and the cult of Osiris in San Francisco witnesses and celebrates its authenticity. She performs the whole herself, with her sister taking parts here and there, evoking by candlelight, by the manipulation of a fan, and by her marvelous voice, a Theater immediate to the imagination, true to the inner vision of the Underworld. Where the old gods preside.

But she who had been the Poet now denies the inspiration of her tunes and next, influenced by certain poetasters and know-betters of the town, seeks to improve the play to suit the dictates of the Stage. She turns against the testimony of the cult of Osiris, holding them insincere or stupid in their praise of the true body, the melodies and plots of the original play to the letter and note. Mr Fair Speech, a prominent member of the Stage Set, and By-Ends, his cousin, persuade her that, for the sake of Production, the Poet's singing voice will not do and must be given over to a hired hack of the theater-world to render in the musical comedy style of the day. Once the magical bloodstream of the music is betrayd, the Ballad key removed, Fair Speech and By-Ends set about further with the writer to fashion the play to their own likes. Now we see that Set has been in it all along.

Puss and Anubis do not appear in the Production, for By-Ends and Fair Speech stand in their place and direct a second play. They will not let the Worm Queen sing, and they alter the plot itself, the sacred mythos. Susan is married to the false bridegroom, crouches in dismay where she is thrown down, rewritten to betray the truth of love for Neil Narcissus' sake, an adulteress to her secret troth. The Worm Queen's command is broken in order to anticipate What-the-Audience-Wants.

But the Worm Queen is the Poet herself, a mask of Isis. The offended Muse blasts the writer with misfortune and cold, kills her beloved cat and touches her heart and mind with despair. The Stage Set sends its Doctor to attend her.

This is all an old story. We realize that not only in the writing but in the betrayal of the play higher orders contend. I am moved to speak, remembering that my own patron, Thoth, has the title He-Who-Decides-In-Favor-Of-Osiris-Against-Set.

Puss-in-Boots, guardian, genius,
  exacting steward too,

of what orders the play,
stands on the right side. But friends,

Mr Fair Speech and By-Ends,
    didnt see it that way and their
        creatures set it over
to their own tune, persuaded her
    to change upon change, against
            inspiration. As in the story
it's always told, these false advisers
    lead the soul astray.

            Anubis stands on the left.

This is how it came to her when she wrote.
    She must have seen them clearly
            and heard
their commanding words. *"The moon is rising.
The moon is setting. Fire! Fire!"*
            they warnd. Each action
of the plot then was in the moon's
    rising and setting. Something's aroused.
            It's settled. The animal fates
do not let us forget. "Watch out!"
    they order. "Do not interfere.
            From every false move
there springs hell's fire."

                The dead
    and the dreamer strive to meet
            in truth, but
their words are changed. They're
    playd false. Wraths of art
            flare from the cat's eyes.
Cold goes out from the ice
    of the Jackal-headed god's stare.

She denies what was reveald.
She tries to play the true Worm Queen,
   but they wont let her sing.
         Her words are changed.

At this stage the Fates are deleted.
   It is all Vanity Fair.
         Neil Narcissus
wants his part rewrit to fit his
   own idea of what he is. Mr Fair Speech
         reproves her protest,
reminds her she owes gratitude
   that they undertake the play at all,
         makes her give way.

The false undertakers, Set's scene fakers,
   make away with the body, cut
         what they dont like and
present the remains in whose likeness?
   Anubis, the fire,
         the passionate dream and true love
are struck from the score.
   Restore the first lines, the scenes
         the way they came to her, the words
as she sings them in the old text!
   The other—
         false face, false pace—false
step by step,
   led by step-relations
         where we should have
watchd our step—
   Satan's pitfall of likelihood
         they'd reshape the plot to,
to take the place of what happend,
   will only
         draw its own to it.

The fun-makers would alter the Maker's
        Will, cut down the fateful
                        orders to psychological size,
humanize Osiris.

We pray against Set:

        Puss-in-Boots, let us obey you.
                Anubis,
                accuse us. Only justice
        will move to restore
                        magic's orders.

        *

                The youngest,
        the Story Teller tells us, *"had
        nothing but the cat"*—
                        The Master Cat heard all
        but, making as if he did not, said
        "Do not afflict yourself."

                        This creation of Charles Perrault,
        this winning surrogate,
                may not be of the older order but
                        Pure Wish or Phantasy. He's
        As-You-Like-It, granted.

        She saw Puss and Anubis
                as automatons,
        marvels of the Musée Méchanique,
                with fans of red and gold, the real
                        directors of what happend.

        By-Ends loth to tell his name,
                Mr Anything, Mr
                        "Facing Bothways,

looking one way and rowing another",
    rearranged the scenes
        to suit his purpose,
saw to it the music would be without meaning.

    Now to get out of this
        "Town of Fair Speech" Bunyan calld it
"If you will go with us," the gods command
    "You must go against Wind and Tide"
        to try the Truth of it.

      *

Susan in the authentic play refuses
    false marriage. She remains
        true to the dream's Truth.
The bridesmaids
    echo the Hangd Man's laugh.
        Satan's words ring.
"Fortunate beauty," they sing. *"Lucky, lucky bride."*
    You should be grateful, you should not
        complain. This share
"fortune and luck" that they even consider
    doing your play—is the Perverter's realm
        "of wealth and pride."

In truth there is an inauspicious star
    as we hear her sing. Only Disaster
        saves her. Susan,
sleepwalking in truth,
    carries the light towards the fire itself.
        The fire
saves her from the lie that threatend.
    Unwed, she dies true to her Love.

    Love and Grief—
only Death grants the deep Wish of the play.
    The lovers in Lethe meet

or in the burning city.
"The man is free of the starry skies,"
    the automaton sings.
"But the woman on earth must wake."

Our Puss in her corner then
    is Sekmet too, lion-wrath of things in full daylight,
        without mercy,
She, whom this lot would betray.

We repeat the prayer,

> *We do not blaspheme the King.*
> *Nor defame Bastet, the Cat-Goddess.*
> *We do not alter the plot.*
> *We do not cavort in the sanctuary.*
> *We do not make fun of your play.*

Let Anubis direct us,
    He who announces Osiris
        restored to full form.

We repeat the prayer to the Lord Accuser.

> *Do not weigh this heart lightly.*

As you workt, we would work
    to bring life to the true body,
        assistant in the magic of Isis,

between earth and high heaven move
    that the place of the god be pure.

        *

The inner voice, the inner
    sight of things, appears, a light
        -ed stage, where

in their closets, Left and Right of What's
    Going On, Going to Happen, we see
        mechanical grotesques.

Gods hide in these—
    "Thrones" the pseudo-Dionysius calld them
        —protagonists,
ideas of the play. They advance the dark thesis
    into daylight. They ask only
        obedience to the letter
and the way will be clear.

    The Divine moves in this Comedy.
        What does she know of these rites
that she did not receive from
    hidden orders
        of laughter and catastrophe?
the writing hand
    following the voice she heard
        in the appropriate melody?

Flatterers, false counselors, fault finders,
    who have her ear,
        always know better
what the stage
    requires—improvements. Envy moves them
        to remove the Divine. What
the audience wants. Vanity
    suggests new arrangements for success.
        "Do not
trust your inspiration," they tell her, "But
    be grateful to *us*.
        We know what works."

They give the play the works. They
    despise her singing as the song came,

persuade her otherwise
to cast out the true measures,
    setting awry
           codes of the angeloi, destroy
tune and tone that kept
    first things in their order.

    Betrayd,
the structures of the poem or play of mind
    (angelic instructions)
        broken,
the genii come to life,
    touch fire to ice in the living bone
        and waken
fearful consequence. They take
    offense who'd promised happiness.
        No part is trivial.
Ravening, they demand exact account in life,
    the message restored.
        The mutilations of the play
are visited upon the other side.

    It was the truth demanded
        we did not know
(they told us) how to work,
    the sequences of the song derived
        from the heart's chord.

  *

In lines so swiftly moving from the hand
    th' elusive phantom is brought out.
        In Lang's *Blue Fairy Book*
Jacomb Hood portrays our Master Cat
    become a great lord.

    We see
that Puss-in-Boots

who in the story has no magic but deceit
preying upon the foolish,
the fearful, the vain, may be
the Wish that betrays what we are,

that like Anubis weighs
the foolish heart, the fearful heart,
the vain heart against
Maāt's feather.

For Hood shows us Puss the Lord
with glaring eyes and

a King's robes.

(Dec. 17, 1961—Feb. 10, 1962)

A SET OF ROMANTIC HYMNS

I

Sweet tone!   Vibrant wing!
Towards-melody-shimmering lure
I'd leap once more

to catch

barb, pang and outpouring

spasm of air

that in the sheen of fish-scale's seen,

            hummingbird's sheath
                    dazzling
            above the gleaming pungent horn

or where the flashing thing's
        sensed in Tiffany's glass, of fire
        and golden life workt to endure,

                to be endured,
        in pure Beauty. What

radiant alliance so that

        like-flame sweep its impulsive skin
                covering the soft infolded brain-
                        meat under the skull,

        shuddering to bear
                adrenalin wave, wing, wonder?

Rush of assent we know to what
        prussian blue and turquoise
                green of the jewel show wakes

the thousand shaking Argus eyes,
        the rustling splendor,
                menacing spears

the human spirit raises in itself
        —armd hosts! This war
        this clamor of bell tongues
                rings round us,
        breaks from Time's keep
                Eternity —a flash!

        Shakings,
rightly, first power over us,

that from the flesh
strike images upon the Orphic lyre.

> The Lover's thighs
> your thighs perform
> melodic torsos
> in the one form
> (nipples are notes).

He turns his head.
He turns progressions of the theme
mercurial. The sound

> follows the muscular lure. His arm
> pit rises from the pit of sound.

The stolen glance,
> the honey-golden
> > leap, the sweeping

changes of keys across the music where
> the body twists as if to return
> > to what shore?

> > As if for song
he smiles. The sweet smile
> steals across the curving lips.

A hand as from the Sun touching.

Vibrant wing! this peril
> in which as towards a secret trust

> > life springs.

Fountain of forms!   Life springs of unique being!

Never again this sequence I am.
Never again this one hand
    drawing its song from men's words.

Never again this one life, this
    universe bent to this lyre
    he would make in the language
            for music's sake.

Never again just this derivation
    from manhood, these numbers,
    this dwelling in the shape of things.

        My Father flies upon the air,
        shakes down black night around me,
        for where I think of him
        his wings are there, his
        crownd eye, his horny beak,
          his lingering cry.

        And from the thought of him I go
        out of all human shape into that pain,
        that crows-skin wizard likeness
        ravaging man most is,
          having a hand in the claw's work,
        the outraging talon
          scraping the hare's bone.

Pure Omen! under the storm cloud

he becomes a bird of the storm.

Burning in the blaze he flies!

III

The lyre's a-blaze!
          And from its burning strings
the children play at making
     music's castles, continents
            and roaring seas,

dig tunnels in the fiery stuff
    to find a meeting of the ways
         underground, to raise
a bridge of things above.

     They labor to refine in their threatend span
     the ancient line of the lyre's curve.

     It was the curve between two horns.

Ivory and Ebony the music ran
from keys that were like crying men.

Red in its courses
the blood in one heart beats.

White and black
hands touch upon the moving keys.

Lips meet in song the Singer always sang.

One man alone plays upon the strings where our hands play.

Do you know where we came from? Do you know where we're
   going?

I only know the way is lonely.

One Lover sings the song the lovers sing.

IV

In praise of Orpheus,
in praise of the Orient,

in the beast's skin
who gave new measures

so that grief came, so that
from the male dance under the hornd head

the chanting voices sang:

> *I have sufferd a great loss.*
> *I turnd and saw her face go out.*
> *I do not remember who she was.*

brought Scythian ways to us,
turnd anew the keys, the strings
shadowd, the rays of Apollo's mode
      alterd,

into whose joyous glare
a burning to the light came
we saw, first dark
pass, then fire within the light,

   new Eros where once
   the woman was.

It was not the Greek way.
It was not the American way.

It was not the way
   Zeus had with Ganymede.
Nor the way brother to brother
   men pledged their troth.
It was not the old fealty.
It increased the need.

It was not the way a man might have
   a change of luck. It was not
   a satisfaction that he brought.
But

changing phrase within the phrase
   so that the voice broke, the notes
      remembering night in the sun's song,
trembling, the hand upon the body shook.

I have sufferd a loss.
I came into manhood estranged from men,

It was a dark way in the light of what was.
It was a changing face.

to sing my Eros,
My Stranger in Love.
I turnd
and caught his wandering glance.

It was a foreign way in a familiar house.

As if there'd been a woman
where I was.

V

The dancers cross over to the other side,
change places and again divide.

She was among the dancers and was not.
The men among the women turn about.

The Sun's gone south.
How many thousands are prepared
to dance Him north?

Shaking bells at each ankle ring,
such sound clusters.
Shaking feathers above the sound sing,
shaking bodies
making configurations of the Sun.

She has gone out among the dancers,
among the persistent figures,
one among a thousand members rememberd.

Vibrant wing!   Everlasting
certainty!

I will always return to this thing,
to the lonely stance,
to the Orphic seizure,
to the loss of my place among the dancers—

and then to the great thousand-ringing moving crowd,
the young men, the fat bucks, the house-wives,
the infants close to their fathers or mothers,
the smiling girls, the chiefs of the tribe,
intent upon the required measures.

As I am, and must be,
intent upon my feet here,
ear cockt to the repeated sound,
that there be the leap up
keep the difference alive in me,

as if I had seen someone,
were about to see someone
in the drift and diversity of many numbers
shifting, in the sameness of
their disresembling—

centrioles form, magnetic poles
of the dancers' ranks in movement.

This is the larva of the Sun.

It's the cry of Marlowe's Faustus that I hear.
    Is *that* a fragment of the song
                impending?   *"I'll leap up . . ."*?

The thousand bells upon their filaments ring.

    "Rend not my heart for naming of my"—

"Christ," he cries. The rime advances.

    The pang's a resonance in all things.

The chromosomes condense into visible threads.
At Santo Domingo the studious indians dance.
                It's Christmas.
In the cold light of the sun
    the Beloved's face goes out.

            The Lover turns.

The Beloved's face is gone.
In loneliness the lyre forms,
          each string
the bracelet of a thousand charms.

          He charms,
bringing accumulations of the sound to rime.

     I sang in the orders of his rime.
     I was most isolate in his charm.

O song of the many changes,
Song of the one thing,

     I have only this song to send

     to take my place among the dancers.

THANK YOU FOR LOVE

(for Robert Creeley)

                              A friend
          's a distant nearness,
          as if it were *my* loneliness you have
          given song to, given a hand

          towards parting without faltering,
          lingering in the touch.

          Is serious grace your part
          in this

tenderness regret enhances?

At the dance we were sad.
Turning aside to talk,
we did not talk but said

what we could say under stars
as they were. Confiding
is a pure gesture, of itself
dear. Towards meeting.

We only referrd to meeting,
a confidence
stumbling has towards moving on.
The feet are there

with us. Given the fact,

we will be moving on.
The song will be moving.
Words are friends
and from their distance

will return.

FROM *THE MABINOGION*

To throw a window open
upon the marges of a sea!

In the closed room
when the party was going
we heard the ocean
out there.

"Look out there!"
the old man warnd the young lords,
"Do not look out there.

"Yesterday is talking upon its sands.
Let it talk on. Do not

look out upon that land
for it is all water
        and washes the shores of this land away."

Do not look
away from this room of no remembrance.
Do not get up from this table,
these trophies, ennuies, celebrations.

Do not turn from this head of a great magic,
filld as it is with wars
and course of retribution after the wars.

To throw a window open!

Time is upon whose naked stretches

    hope roars

we saw the land behind us—

our wastes, our age, our hearts' loss
—and I do not know what we saw:

                this man a wreckt car,
                this man a Lover turn away,
                this man an empty glass upon the bar,
                this man a parody of what he was,

because of our Lord.

That is what the tale says.
That is our adventure.

For I think we've been in
this joint before.

FORCED LINES,

lights in windows of the tall grass,
in whose crusht courses the tramplers lie,
claspt mouth to mouth, speaking

in foreign tongues, thrown down in the
break of the storm to imitate
convulsive images the thunder formd,

given over to strokes of a high weather,

flashes of blue-white
    light in the down-pour,

the striding panic from off shore
    over the sand wastes.

O door flung wide in the way!
O door of seizure, blind impulse
    towards the forced image!

She lay under my weight
drawing me down to drown in the wave

    over us.

Against which excess of what is felt
the discrete poem contends.

"The sprawl" Olson calld such unconsiderd recall of time from its
place into the outwashing provinces of an assumed power.
"That it does this to persons.
And that it damn well has to go
at least from the man of language."

So, Rome or Byzantium lost at its boundaries, consuming
whatever oppositions

—to promote the poem—

thousand-breasted or thousand-culted, thousand-phased
seizure, as if they
might—poets, lovers—mimic the indiscriminate
medium, cross
the line without marking the
change the moon makes.

("It's so nearly finished," Spicer writes me twelve lines back, "that
it scares me that you do anything with it. Only allow yourself
one line (one forced line) and then write a new poem.")

At the moon's teat
having exceeded the excess
an image forced.

A NEW POEM (for Jack Spicer)

You are right. What we call Poetry is the boat.
The first boat, the body—but it was a bed.
    The bed, but it was a car.
And the driver or sandman, the boatman,
    the familiar stranger, first lover,
is not with me.

        You are wrong.
What we call Poetry is the lake itself,
the bewildering circling water way—
having our power in what we know nothing of,
in this having neither father nor son,

our never having come into it,
our never having left it,
our misnaming it, our
giving it the lie so that it lies.

I would not be easy
calling the shadowy figure who refuses to guide the boat
but crosses and recrosses the heart . . .

—He breaks a way among the lily pads.
He breaks away from the directions
    we cannot give—

I would not be easy calling him
    the Master of Truth,
but Master he is of turning right and wrong.

I cannot make light of it.
The boat has its own light.

The weight of the boat
is not in the boat. He will not
give me images but I must
give him images.
He will not give me his name
but I must give him . . .

name after name I give him.
But I will not name the grave easily,
the boat of bone
so light it turns as if earth
were wind and water.

Ka, I call him. The shadow
wavers and wears my own face.

Kaka, I call him. The
whole grey cerement replaces itself and shows
a hooded hole.

From what we call Poetry a cock crows
away off there at the break of something.

Lake of no shores I can name,
Body of no day or night I can account for,
snoring in the throws of sleep I came
sleepless to the joint of this poem,
as if there were a hinge in the ways.

Door opend or closed,
knuckled down where faces of a boat join,
Awake Asleep
from the hooded hold of the boat
join in. The farthest shore is so near
crows fly up and we know it is America.

No crow flies. It is not America.
From what we call Poetry
a bird I cannot name crows.

SONNET 1

Now there is a Love of which Dante does not speak unkindly,
Tho it grieves his heart to think upon men
    who lust after men and run
    —his beloved Master, Brunetto Latini, among them—
Where the roaring waters of hell's rivers
Come, heard as if muted in the distance,
    like the hum of bees in the hot sun.

Scorcht in whose rays and peeld, these would-be lovers
Turn their faces, peering in the fire-fall,
    to look to one another
As men searching for an other
    in the light of a new moon look.

Sharpening their vision, Dante says, like a man
    seeking to thread a needle,
They try the eyes of other men
Towards that eye of the needle
    Love has appointed there
For a joining that is not easy.

SONNET 2

For it is as if the thread of my life
had been wedded to the eye of its needle.

In the sunlight his head
bends over his sewing,

intent upon joining color to color,
working the bedclothes of many cloths.

This patch of Dante's vision in like art
he keeps in Love's name and unites

to the treasured remnant of some velvet shirt.
The flames of the river coupled with the velvet

illustrate the household scene.
He makes it up as he goes along.

It is as if our lives in one thread
had enterd the eye of a lasting need

to begin this work, for this Love
of whom I speak

is not the angel Amor of Dante's song,
tho in him we remember Amor,

but a worker among men
who has taken our lives as one thread

to join as if again
what we see in what we have never seen.

SONNET 3

From Dante's Sixth Sonnet

Robin, it would be a great thing if you, me, and Jack Spicer
Were taken up in a sorcery with our mortal heads so turnd
That life dimmd in the light of that fairy ship
The Golden Vanity or *The Revolving Lure,*

Whose sails ride before music as if it were our will,
Having no memory of ourselves but the poets we were
In certain verses that had such a semblance or charm
Our lusts and loves confused in one

Lord or Magician of Amor's likeness.
And that we might have ever at our call
Those youths we have celebrated to play Eros
And erased to lament in the passing of things.

And to weave themes ever of Love.
And that each might be glad
To be so far abroad from what he was.

ANSWERING

(after CLARITAS by Denise Levertov)

> A burst
> of confidence. Confiding
>
> a treasured thing
>
> kept inside,
> as if it were a burden,

worrying about money,
or were pride
and ambition struggling—

sings out.

It was a song I did not sing.

*

The men are working in the street.
The sound

of pick and pneumatic drill

punctuates
the chirrup a bird makes,

a natural will
who works the tossing dandelion head

—a sheaf of poems.

They are employd
at making up a joyous

possibility.

They are making a living
where I take my life.

*

With no more earnest skill
than this working song

125 ✴✴✴✴✴✴

sings
—as if the heart's full

responsibility
were in the rise of words

as momentarily
that bird's notes he concentrates

above the swaying bough,
the fluttering wings.

*

For joy
breaks thru

insensible to our human want.
Were we birds too

upon some blowing crown of seeds,
it would be so

—we'd sing as we do.

The song's a work of the natural will.
The song's a work of the natural will.

ADAM'S WAY

A PLAY UPON THEOSOPHICAL THEMES

PERSONS IN THE CAST

Adam	Mrs Maybe
Erda-Eve	
	Angels:
Dragons:	Michael
Hermes	Samael
Lilith	

Tree-shadows:
Pook
Bobbin

SCENES

1. The Astral Garden.   A Séance
2. Eden.   The Garden of Yahweh

From the dark before the play Adam *appears as speaker of the prologue:*

> I've seen a girl just now. Erda,
> Maid of the Wood, they calld her.
>
> Two guys were with her, Pook and Bobbin.
> I've seen them before
> at the corner of my eye.
>
> You look aslant and talk to yourself
> and you'll see them
> —that's the kind they are—

127 ::::::::::

clear as you please,
whether it be dark or daylight.

I saw her there today for the first time
and I know now that hers is the real world
and it is real in her.

> I've seen a girl and tho
> I know not who I am
> I know now what I am
> for I am this girl's lover
> and am no more.

He disappears into the dark. Stage lights rise, disclosing the astral or dream forest which extends in time as it extends in space an other world of wish, or it is the interior of a shaman's tent, for its forms are stylized. We see the masks of trees and paths, as we hear masks of speech, that only the man of childish imagination may go along with us. To the left the dragons Hermes *and* Lilith *enter, moving from back to front stage and turning upon their steps again, weaving a path along a fissure in time from some catastrophe in the reptilian past into the mind of near-man. They seem to push their way, as if step by step against stages of the resisting air, blindly, for they move in their own dark we do not see but know in their moving, until they break thru into the elves' world, hearing first and then seeing, as if they broke thru the shell of an egg.*

Hermes   For days we have wanderd in this wood
         with no more light to go by
         than if we went by the mind's light.

Lilith   We have not been going by night or day
         but by a dream's time
         led astray from our true ends.
         What do we know of the sun? We may be underground
         for all we know of the sky's light.

Hermes	It filters down
	thru worlds above of dust and leaves.
	It loses itself amidst the dusky twitterings of . . .
	birds I suppose they are up there.

Lilith	In great Atlantis the Sun did shine
	and wed the Moon to make night and day.
	The city I loved was like the sky
	whose princes were stars of that nuptial bed.

Hermes	These are things you dream of that have never been.
	If pity could move the world above,
	it would release your mind from this bond
	to what it has lost and make a place of the dead.
	We have known nothing for sure but the Flood.

The elf-shadows Pook *and* Bobbin *and the earth-daughter* Erda *are seen now dimly, moving in a dance of forest-lights that broadens and takes over the stage as they begin to speak. The dragons move more cautiously, as if they were coming upon something, and the elves, feeling the presence of intruders, dance with their unease.*

Lilith	Dead? Dead? There was no flood.
	It was but the flooding of our fear.
	Atlantis is not dead. It is but dark
	and will return.

Hermes	Wait! I think I hear voices here.

Pook	I waver today
	as if a man were looking at me
	and I were changing shape
	the way we do in men's eyes.

Erda	I prefer bees
	who have nothing to do
	with what's calld men.

                    In their minds I am so small
                        I ride upon their hairy backs
                and climb into the shaking calyxes of things.

                        Or with the wind I'll go,
                            a thought in the weather moving trees,
                    and blow about despite what men are,
                            invisible to their sight of what is.

Bobbin   Yet whenever they see us
             we must look like men,
             for men see not what things are but what
             they are in things.   The world changes
             dark to light as their eyes change.

Hermes   Surely these are voices talking near at hand.
             I cannot understand what they are saying.
             There are words I almost hear, yet it is all
             no more than a baffled conversation
             beyond a wall.

Lilith   We may be close
             upon a crack in such a wall
             between this world and another world.

             At certain fissures in time I heard,
                  before Atlantis fell,
             bells of the last days ring
             as if sounding in a flood, and I knew not
             what they were or what they told.
             Bending towards a point in the air
             —it seemd no more than that—
             until the blood rang in my ears
             I almost overheard . . . such voices.

Hermes   Hush! They are here.

Erda   Not I!
                        I stir their thoughts
                        until they are like
             whirlpools in the water and no longer
                        resemble themselves.

Pook	Ah, Erda! What's a man? You are so free of it it almost seems *we* might be free.
Bobbin	They see us as gods they have discarded, as little men, urchins, shaggy dwarves— or, when they are most enamord of evening, before their eyes we ride lords and ladies in a host.
Erda	Everything they think materializes. The Sun they've thought a physical thing, a burning mass. The Earth's grown solid and substantial in their sight of it. And Paradise, that was a bubble where images whirld, they burst in order to know it all. The rest is grit and oil.
Pook	Is ours the Earth? or is their earth Earth?
Bobbin	Our Earth is Erda where she goes.
Hermes	The air is turning upon itself to let us through. Come, Sister, into this opening of the way.
Pook	There *are* men about. It makes even Erda thicken and we think of them.
Bobbin	They've lost their moon I've heard. It went dead on them they knew so much about it. What this *knowing* is must be a terrible thing. It breaks their world to atoms in their minds.
Erda	Their gods in knowing leave their stories and lose hold. So this god Moon fell. It was a falling down of Man from his own story into a thickening of time.

131 ░░░░░░░

Hermes	We must be near. They speak now
	in our own tongue or we have taken on their ears.
	"Gods", "knowing", and then
	the words "Moon" and "Man" I heard.

Lilith   They know something of the Moon?

Hermes   Here they are. I see them now.

Now Hermes *stands at the "door" and the whole stage becomes the forest-shadow world, for the dragons had unwound their world along the path they followd.*

Hermes, *addressing the elves:*

> We feard the Moon of which you speak
> was gone. It's been
> as if we were underground
> in tunnels of the Sun in the Night World.
> We came thru some passage we could not see
> but moved along a feeling we had. And then
> I heard you speaking of gods and of the Moon
> we thot had fallen from the sky.
> For we would see the Moon in hope
> that what we know was all a dream
> and that the gods still rule.

| Pook | Gods! We know no gods! |

| Lilith | Except Darkness. |

Bobbin	The mirror in the sky has fallen down
	and every man's soul's his own.
	I'd as soon have a stye in my eye
	as be looking for a god.

| Lilith | Darkness is a god. |

Hermes	My sister was priestess of the Moon
	at the Great Abyss before Atlantis fell.
	But now she has only a confused memory of that fall
	and dwells in phantasy of the time before,

denying change.
I myself, like her, am Child of the Moon.
But there was no Moon when I was born.
She and I seem to be in some ellipse of time,
there being no measure of Man where there is no Moon.

Pook   Moon, who knows Moon?
Moo of the cows I know
and oon of the wind,
for I have heard it
herding the kine before the sun.
But Moon I have not heard nor seen.

Erda   There is a chapel in this wood
I've heard of—a green place . . .

Bobbin   My grandfather knew stories of this
—"Moon" you call it.
The thing hung but a mile up they said,
and there were men, another race,
made music as if to play it down
or caught reflections of whatever it was
in pools. It was a pool itself
of light or blood. They do say both.
But it fell,

and that's what Hell was.
It was all stone and ice.

Erda   . . . There's an old dame there
who calls herself Moonmère.
For Moon's her son.

Bobbin   What falls like that will never rise again
but whirls in its own dust to sting men's eyes.

Lilith   It was not the Moon then. The Moon did not fall.
There was no ice, no glassy shards, no
falling out. We did not have a falling out.

133 ✺✺✺✺✺✺

She but hid behind the appearance of the sun
and will be back again when he is done.

Hermes   I've heard the rumor there were other Moons,
                    early ages of what Man now is.
     And that those who belongd to the first Moon's time
                    were born from eggs
     and died spawning in tides of the summer seas.

     They had no bones. Their eyes were feelers.
                    And yet they were
                    men like us.

Pook   The glacier rubbd smooth all that constituate roughness
     that made *us* kind of men. Whatever was human
     fled long ago South and West, before the Hyperborean
        blast
                  and we're what's left.

Lilith   If this be so, how do these
     green plants and flowering trees survive?
     For days we've walkt in this wood
     —it may be for years or centuries.
     I remember nothing but this shade, these corridors
     of ancient trunks and branches overhead.

Bobbin   Deluded woman! Do you not know
     this is a place stript by the glacial mass,
     a mirror of glassy stone? These are
     but green reflections of what once was,
     cloudy simulations of departed trees.
     We live in a forest of the primeval shadow,
     and we are shadows of men upon a polisht stone.

Lilith   The Moon is a great seed. This I knew
     when in Atlantis we would move
     mountains slowly by the persistent force
     life has in any little seed. The seed of man,
     that swells into the egg of things he sees,

from its ache casts phantoms of what he does not see
—such as *you* are now,

[*she dismisses* Pook *and* Bobbin *who vanish into the growing shadows and leave the stage, followd by* Hermes]

> dwellers you say
> where there is no Moon, seedless men.

> We have come to a place then where
> birth and death have been erased,
> for there is no generation without this
> Mistress of all Seed calld Moon.

[Lilith *exits, and* Erda *stands alone upon the stage*]

Erda   There is a chapel in the wood I know of, a green place
            sacred to the Moon whose seed is Man.
            The ancient Chatelaine keeps a bower there
            of thorns one time wherefrom roses in their
                 first nature burst,
            flare their curling petals wide
            and fall aside from their dark hips,

                or then again this Vine
            is of so various an impulse sprung
              a climbing pulse it seems,
            flowering in a rhetoric of violet, blue, pink,
            effusing a sweet crowded perfume upon the air
            that's music to the rising sense of smell,
              an orphic lure to nostrils come,

            so that eyes and ears, confused, drink in
              the rampant musk
            that draws the elemental spirits round like bees
            where clusterd genitals of the honeysuckle bloom
              are crusht.

The dreams that from the groins of such
      leafy seclusions go abroad
are larvae from which seductive forms
confused the purposes of God and broke
      from Adam's side a body for Eve.

The Pod this vegetable Dame calls her Cabinet.
      Adam again and again, unbroken,
unriven from his green womb returns.

      All the lovely promise of the blossoms
goes to pieces, attackt by swarming spirits,
      nymphs of a summer rapture,
and the swelling pods hang down,
      heavy with new men.

We fairies are immortal, and there are
human souls so ancient that as babes
they look with eyes of lizards they were once
who out of love tear flesh from flesh.
There are such men, old with more than centuries,
so that the ravening forces of the old sea
      roar in the ears of many a child;
      and this is a continuity of woe.

But ah! the green woe! the fresh
suffering, the ever new souls
this relentless creatrix looses upon the world!

The stage is now dark and Erda *is gone.* Adam *and* Samael *enter with the seed-pod of the vegetable Man, which is also the cabinet of the medium. A séance table and four chairs are set up down stage left where* Michael *takes his place in the dark with his back to the audience.*

Mrs Maybe *enters with a lit kerosene lamp which she sets on the table, taking her place opposite* Michael, *facing the audience, and begins laying out her cards, talking to* Michael *as Colonel Perkins as she goes.*

Mrs Maybe   These cards aint Tau Roots.
               They's my own signs, Colonel Perkins.
               I get them in dreams from a China man
                       who before this time
               was a spreading mass in Mu of gelatinous wisdom.

               Adam, dont let yourself nod that way!
               If you fall asleep tonight
               we may never fish you out.

Adam   I dont know what to say in here.
               I havent got my lines.
               Am I supposed to listen?

Mrs Maybe   Dont be silly. You just say what comes to you.
               This is only an entertainment.
               It dont make any difference until *you* make it.

               The white card is up tonight,
               the frying pan with eyes.
               and here's the ivy-coverd well.
               The flying thing above's a hen.

               Your lines will come, Adam.
               Be patient.

               We've got our own game of Patience to play.
               This card is something like the Moon in tarrots.
               The Baboon's Bottom I call it.

               That boy's green, Colonel.
               He's either dozing off or he's straining.
               But how the flies gather round
               it dont compare.

               The boy's got an aura
               no more than a seedling plant.

               The old ones come to a green youngster like that
               hoping for some first bud of a leaf or

137

sput of a flower, like a child goes
for a first star at evening.

And here's the motorbus.
Dont it look ominous standing there
with no one in it like that!
Waiting or left over, who's to know?

Is it the windows with no faces
or the seats with no bodies
that gives a person such a turn to see it?
Ready to start or end of the line!

Adam!   [*Rappings answer from the cabinet*]
        He's started rapping.

[Lilith *and* Hermes *enter from the audience, taking their places now
as Mrs Webb and friend at the séance table*]

                They'll soon be with us.
        The shoe in the ice-flow!
        A dark symbol that, Colonel Perkins.
        Brings a chill over a body
        playing solitaire.

Lilith   What was in the cards tonight?

Mrs Maybe   I was just telling the Colonel.
            A play between this side and the other side.

Hermes   I feel a draft along my back.

Mrs Maybe   Our audience in their Summerland
            feels you out and finds you are not real.

[*We hear rappings again from the cabinet, and* Samael *and* Adam
begin to speak, imitating each the other]

Samael   Are you there?

Adam	There's someone here would speak to you.
Hermes	To who?
Lilith	To *whom*.
Samael	I cant get a line.
Adam	The line wont come thru.
Mrs Maybe	Mrs Webb, stop rocking the table. Let it rock by itself.
Hermes	I see a green light over the closet.
Mrs Maybe	Stop seeing things and let the scene begin.
Samael	I cant get a line.
Michael	The line breaks at times like this because of what the author dares not say or fears we'll say. It's a party line. He interferes with what we are. Then we've to take things by the ears and start some automatic talk ourselves. Let rhetoric be our cabinet and Mrs Maybe here will sit inside. Adam, our sensitive, is green. We found him out and stole him from a show we'd seen in town.
Mrs Maybe	And there's an impersonator if I ever saw one I said. Mention the Moon and that boy will go into his phases. There is no part he'll not try on if it comes to him. Right now he's caught the way the scene is balking and he balks.
Lilith	An amateur! We came to see the real thing, and now we're askt to wait upon this amateur!

Hermes	She means some occult lesson by all this.
	I felt it when we arrived tonight
	and I was right. The temperature was cold
	and the color was green.

Mrs Maybe	When things go like this
	I cut the cards and call it Patience.
	Fish around in this water
	and the fish will come.
	The Tibetans call it the Bardo state.
	With only that cabinet
	between ourselves and the play.

If you'll give in a bit,
the thing will move.
I've been told by my masters there's a play tonight
      whatever we say.
You two want something great
—a lesson from beyond or a spirit light—
or something funny—a creaking door.

You block my way.

[*She turns down the lamp. The light for the astral scene appears again.* Erda, Pook *and* Bobbin *enter rear scene by the cabinet*]

Erda	Are you there?
	O Mother Moon, Moonmère!
	We've come to see the Son
	you told us of
	that men call Moon.

Mrs Maybe	The light we see you by, my dear,
	is the Moon's light.
	We see you by the light you are.

The Son you seek is dark.
He sits inside his green bower
at a loss for words.

He's seen his bride-to-be,
a shadow in his mind's eye,
and that is all the light he knows.

Erda   How is there Moon's light without Moon?
You say he's in the dark.

Mrs Maybe   Love-light, Love-light.

Pook   Dont listen to the witch.
I knew those dragons asking for the Moon
would ruin things. What's Man
that he would have our Erda as his own
and rob the shadows for his light?

Erda   Yet when I heard her say
"the light you are" I felt
all light . . .

Bobbin   We'll hide you, Erda,
in another likeness.
And if he's seen *us* too,
we'll wear another face.

Beware the green Man or Moon
who has need of us.
Let us tear this pod open
before he's ripe.

Erda   . . . I felt all
light, and alien to myself.

What is love-light?
As if Erda were a solitude.

Pook   Let's rip him out
before his time begins.

Bobbin   Leave him exposed, unfinisht as he is!
            [*he listens at the cabinet*]
There's not a sound in there.

141

Erda [*alone*]:

His name is Change.

I heard the names of Man
ring down the chambers of a dream,
as if from round to round
of that great shell Time is, where
elves and shadows build eternal halls,
Moon and Man and Woman out of Man
rang Change and Change
and Night was figured with a soul.

His name is Hell
and Heaven too. I heard the names of Man
boom in every cell as if it were
a waiting room where frightend creatures
stood at bay before
a door in creation or at
the breaking of some day, a dragon's egg.

His name is Love.
And, What is Love? I said.
I heard the creaking of a step
and heard the beating of a heart.
All innocence from its shade had fled.
All single being was torn apart.

Pook   Tear down the bloody cabinet.
This pod's a throne where there was no throne.

Bobbin   God has grown tired of His green flourishing.
He dreams no longer happy in His night
because of this thing.
Erda heard his name was Change.

Tear the walls of this magic down
before his sleep ripens and he wakes a king.

Pook *and* Bobbin *tear down the cabinet, revealing* Adam, *who falls out inert like a doll, and* Samael, *who stands motionless as if unseen.* Pook *stares into* Adam's *face.* Bobbin *listens at his chest.*

Bobbin   He's not alive!
                He's dead! He's dead!
                He will not ripen.
                There's not a sound in here.

Pook   There's not a breath
                nor any light in his eye.
                He was not born. He will not die then.
                He did not happen.

Erda   O how sad! For now
                there will be no shadow of him.
                What kind of a thing is this then?
                Great God's a doll
                and what I thought was a heart in me
                stands still.

Bobbin   Come away! Come away!
                We've undone fate
                and there'll be no
                changes of the Moon tonight.
                Nature's a tower has been torn down.
                Man's but a doll, and all that
                fearful restless thought is done.

[Pook *and* Bobbin *exit with* Erda. Mrs Maybe, Michael *and* Samael *move from their places to stand over* Adam's *body where it lies.*]

Mrs Maybe   He was shaped in the heart of nature
                and there must find his place.

Michael   He was shaped in the light of what was
                and must face what has not been.

Samael   He was shaped in the dark of thought
                and will come to himself in time.

Mrs Maybe   As if there were an age of no moon
              there being neither birth nor death,
              he was deliverd untimely from the womb.

Michael   They brought him forth. They knew not
              what they did. The fates
              were undone. There is now only faerie.

Samael   The work of this night is fair to see.
              What we could not do these wights have done.
              They have set free what they but heard of
              in the confusions of a dream and feard.
              Another round of God is sprung.

Mrs Maybe   Our gifts remain.
              The lock's thy smile. The key's a kiss.
              And thou, unknowing, will see thy soul.

Michael   This is the instruction of the Sun.
              When from your self you are undone
              What thou truly art will be begun.

Samael   Love from the left side I bring.
              This is the double cross of the Sun.
              So that Man may be a king.

              Between you and thee
              such a separation and yearning as between
                    hell and heaven,
              bound to be free, free to be bound,
              until thou turnest all things to thy burning.

[*They turn from the scene.* Samael *exits.* Mrs Maybe *and* Michael *resume their places at the séance table.* Adam *rises and takes his stance for a soliloquy.*]

Adam   What a relief to get out of that green bag.
              I had to sit in there with the devil breathing down my
                    neck,

with the whole cast talking poetry, "Moon" and "Man",
and nothing to say myself but about how
I didnt know what to say and how I hadnt got my lines.

Now you find out I'm Adam for sure or
    something like that,
and everybody says I'm a green nut
    before there ever was a tree.

Those elves break open the shell I'm in like a pea-pod
    and I fall out, brought forth unborn.
As if there had been a Man in the beginning
    who didnt know Life or Death or anything,
having neither Breath nor Heartbeat.
And Gods or Fairy Godfathers and Mothers
    standing over him with three gifts or wishes,
as if he were an early version of Sleeping Beauty.
He's not supposed to wake or speak
until some Princess kisses him and breaks the spell.

Well, a Man's more than that.
Those Dragons, Mother Maybe or Nature or
    whoever she may be,
the Angels and Fairies—they can say all kinds of things
but I'm given no soliloquy.

My author is afraid of me.
Doesnt he come himself at dawn
kissing people and announcing day?
He's afraid I'll go after Bobbin or Pook
or the Lady Dragon before I'm thru
and betray the image in which I'm made.
But that's the way a Man is
    if he's let go.
Michelangelo drew his Author—mine's the same—
    reaching out so
to touch poor Adam's extended finger in a game
    calld "Pass-the-Soul", no doubt.

Now I tell you there's no gesture
that's not part of the plot of such a God.
He's afraid to lose face in me.
He'll not reach out of place, but I
must find Him out in all the indirections of the plot.
He has no place to reach except in me.

You'll see. This Eden he devises
is no happy thought, but divides us,
him and me, from what we really are about.

Seald between the lips and kiss
the world is stilld. We dream. We fear to wake.

[Adam *lies back, returning to his dream*]

We dream and, sightless, cast reflections
each in each as in a lake,
above, below, a mountain appears.

Hermes   What is the meaning of this
presentation that would be Man?
Where are we then? Are we not men?
If this be Man that we have seen, unborn,
yet speaking so before the beginning of his world,
then we've come to a time that's not our own.

What is my face like, Sister? It's grown strange
to me in a fear I have. Was I once
in God's high image made and then put aside
that this thing here is the race of Man?

I feel my sight, heavy as stone, as if
in the changes of time I were cast down.
Your eyes are a snake's eyes, and it seems
we have a serpent likeness you and I
for I remember where we went
the sound of scrabbling claws upon dry ground.

Mrs Maybe   O.K. Let me hold a mirror to your—"soul"
I'd say, but your soul has had its day.

You were once what you are not now.
In seas of the first earth you bathed
and you were Man before Man was.

You were fluid then, a network of soul,
        spread for miles about,
breaking and remaking itself in waves.
God and Nature broke and remade themselves in you.

All this fluid Being was calld Atlantis
and it was a moving thing. And in its movement
the dream calld Man was hidden. Your kind
ravend to come into their own.
They fed their souls, their Manhood, to a demon moon
to bind God and Nature to their will.

Lilith   Then God's grown small if He'd survive
in this little thing we see tonight as Man.
And we are all that's left
of God's hugeness in the ancient world.

Now I remember the million islands,
I remember the slumbering cells,
when Eden drifted upon the tides
and all the land was fiery hell.

I remember the heaviness when it came.
I remember the net closing, the million gathering,
the dragon gel in the angry sea,
the spectral moon above the flood
that shadowd earth in storm and night.

Ringd round with auras of the raging sun
above the watery waste I saw
        the winged disc spread out
bleeding from flaming seas above
when first into this world I came.

Was there a time when in the tides of stars I was
back of memory a more protean dispersion of my self?

147 ✲✲✲✲✲✲

before this scene of a passionate universe
    drew me down
into the heart-beat of a single star?

In the greatness of time there was a wedding,
a power, a ring between the earth and sun,
a radiant bond in which we were borne
upon a wave of wonder in the world,
Atlantis, where God in His Glory came.

It shrinks. The memory shrinks.
I feel the stiffening of a spine.
The warmth I knew is black and cold in me now.
Atlantis, the broken ring, is gone,
and all our will crawls underground.

Hermes   Then our faces are masks thru which we look
with eyes that now will never find alive
the fires from which our kind have come.
God has gone on and left us behind among old ways,
and we lay our eggs in wastes of sand
that were once the sea.

                From crevices
of primal memory we creep upon the earth again,
no longer ours, only to see   this-s-s
image has usurpt our place.

The ring of serpent isles Poseidon kept
is gone, and Eden is an orchard now,
a field of grass-s-s   from which
new rivers run.

Lilith   The Author of our race has put us away
and shaped this thing of clay in a new image
    to take our place.
As if He were dissatisfied
and could perfect Himself by Art from life and death,
He's made this Garden out of time,

an Eden of His eternal thought,
an orchard having the grace of many trees.

So that in an other Garden kept Above
the Ancient of Days who was a serpent
walks in a new guise of Man and would be at peace
because of this Work of His Art Below.

This Doll is a thing we must curse
        and most contemn.
For all the ancient War is still, in him.
The contending powers in which our glory swelld
no longer contend, and we are driven underground.

Some part of God's then driven underground.
And only a divided Being has amused Himself
with this puppet likeness Adam is.

"The lips are lockt, the key's a kiss"
I heard great Nature say.
And from the chambers of my despisèd heart
I heard the oldest wisdom hiss-s-s,
"The agony of Creation will not be done.
The ancient War is still in him."

[*The stage lights dwindle and* Mrs Maybe *turns down her lamp during the following speech until, beginning with the words* "Night and her powers", Lilith *is in total darkness*]

Lilith   Now the secret whereby Atlantis came to grief
returns to my fury the Power we found.
It was the undoing of the Seed,
the splitting of the knots in the nets of God.

Before the first spark appeard
and from its kindling heart of light
pourd forth its treasure into elemental fire,
into the worlds and all the images of what we are,
there was a Dark of God from which He came.

Night and her powers, the Death behind our deaths,
the Silent Invisibles of the Great Abyss
and the chilling Wing that casts despair, grief,
terror upon all living things—these
but hint of what   God's first Emptiness is.

[*She passes now into the region where* Adam *lies, standing at his
boundary to evoke in him God's void.*]

Lilith   Back of the burning of the fire,
              back of His yearning,
                    the Void He Is.

              Back of the show, the images, the Epiphany,
                    the Void He Is.

              Back of the act, the incarnation, the passion,
                    the Void He Is.

[*After a prolongd silence,* Lilith, *as if echoing, sighs in anguish*
a-a-a-a-a-a. *Now all but unbearable silences, designated by three
periods* . . . , *open between* Adam's *questions that follow and*
Lilith's *answers. The whole scene has the inertia of nightmare.*]

Adam   Who is there? . . .

Lilith   Darkness . . .

Adam   Who is there? . . .

Lilith   Woman . . .

Adam   Who is there? . . .

Lilith   Lilith . . .   The Door . . .

Adam   What door is calld Lilith? . . .

Lilith   The Door Without is the same as the Door Within . . .

Adam   To where? . . .

Lilith   To the Void . . .
                    Beyond the empty feeling you have . . .

Adam   [*in anguish*]   O, O! Where am I? . . .

Lilith   You are neither in life nor in death . . .

Adam   I suffer . . .

Lilith   You are dreaming . . .

Now she moves slowly over him, keeping the nightmare pace of the scene, and covers him in the embrace of the incubus, awakening him with her kiss to her own emptiness. After long pause, she rises and begins to retreat, and her voice and her silences come as echoes of what they were.

Adam   What am I dreaming? . . .

Lilith   The lips are lockt. The key's a kiss-s-s . . .

Adam   Are you my soul? . . .

Lilith   Before the soul, I was-s-s . . .

Adam   My lips are parted. What is this? . . .

Lilith   A kiss-s-s . . .

Adam   A tongue darted
within my mouth.
What poison's this? . . .

Lilith   [*exiting*]   Time's kiss-s-s . . .

The stage light has changed as it comes on from the astral light of the forest to the full light of Eden-side. Erda enters.

Erda   I thought I heard Moon cry out.
Perhaps the thought of him cried out in me.
I cannot always tell the thought in the world
from the world in thought, for there are
moods that are all weather I would not know
were it not for clouds racing, swept up clean

151 :::::::::

from an horizon with trees dancing high
in the blue air. O now,

this one they call Moon or Man
is a mood in me. [*turning to Adam where he lies*]
        Can you hear?

It is as if he were fast asleep.
Yet he's not alive Pook said.
And he's not dead. How has he happend then?
For he has happend to me.

His lips seem almost to smile.
O almost smiling lips, are you
on an edge of being alive?   [*Erda kneels by Adam*]

How gentle he looks! I'll kiss him now
before he looks, as if it were
lips of the sunlight upon his lips.

[*She kisses him, then springs up saddend and turns away*]

O! He does not see or hear me.
What a heavy light love-light must be.
Pook and Bobbin wanted to rescue me from this.
That's why they broke him from his place, unripe.
But my heart's his place,
and the time was ripe, I fear.

He does not stir, yet the sight of him
stirrd in me when he was not there
and made a heart.

It's as if I had been taken from his side
and, coming back now to look at him,
came home.
      O Moon,
now Erda's not her own,
but Man and Change and Fear   [*Enter* Samael]
    are her masters.
Moon Mother was right.

It's by your light   [*Enter* Michael]
that Erda would have her being and be seen.

Samael Eve.
Not Erda, but Eve.
Not Moon, but Man.
Adam is his name.
Not Fear, but Fire.
Love is the nature of the Change.
His name is Adam.
By his light
you will know love.
By your love
he will be light.

Erda-Eve Eve? Adam?

Michael Eve-Adam you were before the play began,
our Author's image here below
in which He has created
new orders Above. I have here
a letter describing the turn of the play:

As Erda you were but a fancy
and moved playfully at your-His whim.
Yet there was a dance in this
of another form in correspondences.

You were a rib of substance in Adam's dream.
He was a rib of spirit in your play.
Perhaps our Author intended first
there would be no wedding in the universe
between the image and the sound of things
but moulded the lovely form of Man
inert and perfect in one Art
and surrounded that substantial form
with an invisible calld music, calld "Erda",
an air or melody previous to its element,
a flowering fragrance of a thought to come.

153 ✼✼✼✼✼✼

It was our Author's delight
        so to illustrate Himself
in disparate Arts.   But now,

seeing a certain beauty in His work,
        between the vision and the song,
He's moved to try the magic of a realm
—Eden, the marriage before Heaven and Hell.

Eve you are now and most will be in Adam.
As he will find himself and freedom in you
from his original elements released
into the innocent melody of a higher law.

As Eve, you are Imagination's child. Wife-man,
        woman you are.
Erda no longer of air alone but of earth too.
This air more than air. This earth
more than earth, in you.
        Womb-man of Adam's life.

[*Addressing Adam*]   Up, Adam!   Awake!   Wake up!
        Eve has risen from your side.
        The door upon your life's flung wide in the way.
        Do you not feel the kiss
                of morning's light upon your lips?

        The Night is done. From your base elements
        you are removed, and Day's your bride.

Adam   [*stirring up from his Night-World, as if to himself*]
        Woman? Woman? What venom's this? Day's kiss?

Samael   Ah, there was a woman and a kiss in the Night,
        I see.

Eve   O darling Moon, O Adam,
        wake for me!
        I feel as if I'd been asleep in him
        and now, if only from his passing dreams he wakes,
        I wake with him to one great lasting dream.

Adam [*continuing in soliloquy*]: I've been asleep
                        and would have slept the play away,
                        talking brave things according to the dreaming will
                        and seeing all the secret scenes
                        behind what the eye sees. A man can see there
                        what is only a word in this
                        here world and hear
                        what men awake but see.

                        I felt the dragon cold of age, and I am young.
                        I saw figures of a song as fairies dancing
                        and heard the fates romancing over me
                        what plots I cannot remember for the life of me
                        and then—saw Death in what I could not see.

Samael   Death too, *before* Immortal Life, it seems
                        came in this Night's dreams.

Michael   Let these things be calld Dreams of the Night
                        and be no more than that, but put away
                        the schemes such primal matters weave,
                        things seen by closed eyes and heard
                        by the oppresst ears, there being here,
                        by Day's light, neither sight nor sound of them.

                        For this is Life, and morning's come.
                        This place is Eden-side. And you are of Eden now,
                        seed of the Sun. Obey the magic of this place.
                        Your bride is Life—Eve—even now before you here
                        that our Author to bring you to life
                                has taken out of you.

                        I have here too the warnings of this Art.
                        It is the other side of a grievous fear
                        and God has put His heart in the balance
                                of your obedience:

                        All things in happiness have been contrived
                        thru Eve. She is the Mother of all things.

Of all the trees of this garden you may eat.
Of this tree alone you may not eat.

In sun and rain and the common earth,
in every plant and each and all the creatures round about
you may grow into the fullness of your Self,
for these are Eve, in Her
       —but not in yourself.
Obey Love as it first springs in the sight of her
so that all the universe is loved and everywhere
you would be the servant of every life therein.
This is the keeping of this place.
This is the law of Eden.

Adam   How may I grow into what I do not know?
If I am a self in all that is not me,
I am all darkness to myself.

Samael   You will not grow into yourself easily.
This is your last green season. You need not
trust this magic, for it has too much
need of you. There is a reason the Sun has
       sent you this messenger.
He brings you news that I too can tell you of.
For every thing he means to instruct you in
I'll show you in an other way
and help you win his purpose for your own.
Then keep God's balance if you will.

In the first place, when that place was Eden,
He and I brought into man's giant ancestral identity
       a single ray
and Adam-Who-Was became a seed of many seeds,
a race of all God's trouble in the world.

That first Man contain his Sun
as if it were a part of Him. Nothing was,

apart of Him. He loomd in all the universe.
There was no outline of such a Man.

This is the Adam that you know in dreams.
And from such a World-Man each morning you wake,
as now in Eden, as if Day were true,
and shake your head as if the thought of Him
would prove you false.

Hell and Heaven were no more
than dispositions of His bowels.
Eve was a rib the oldest riddles say.
And Purgatory unawakend breathed in the balance
        of what he was.

Michael   This demon who addresses you
speaks just that portion of the truth
that we must consider to be untrue to happiness.
For Eden is a magic you must keep.
It is the light of a law from which a shadow falls.
Before this light was, there was no shadow-side.

Before I was, *he* was not.
There was one shot in the dark of light
that coming into the gravity of what Man was
broke down or fell out with itself
into a daimon and a demon of the Sun.

I am the One. He is the Other.
I would tell the truth of Eden-side.
He other wise.

Samael   Aye, Truth is Eternal.
My brother here in Truth speaks true.
The Truth he knows is partial to one side of things.
There is no truth in time
that does not fall or split apart
to rime with some fiction of itself,
insincere to its original nature,

but chases after the possibility of a
like sound as if it were a fact
in some transcendent magic He'd call Good.
Thus Poetry most resembles the works of things
and Adam must find himself in Eve.
                              [*Exit* Michael *and* Samael]

Adam   If you would tell me who I am
            —devil or angel, I don't care—
            I'll play Man, if that's my name.

            I came from such a green stillness
            into this life, I must have a name to come.
            And in a dream I do not remember, I saw
            the face I do not remember of one I love.

[*He turns to face* Eve]

Eve   Was she fearful?

Adam   She was most like you. She was everywhere.
            Come closer here. Your name is Eve?

Eve   My name is as you wish. Eve, yes.

Adam   Were you ever another? Erda? Maid of the Wood?

Eve   Before you, I was ever an other.

Adam   You were everywhere.

Eve   Yes, I was everywhere.

Adam   And I understand then what our Author means,
            for you are all the trees in the garden,
            and were it not for you
            I alone would be the one tree and not
            be Adam. Now in your eyes I see the tree is fair
            in which I lose myself thru you.

Eve   There's a way of speaking that's most like this
            where thought and feeling is not our own
            but belongs to a voice that would transmute

into a music joy and grief, into one living tree
in which beyond our selves we find release.

"Rime" the demon calld it and made a wry face
as if it were wrong
where words are obedient to song's measure
        beyond our will.
But the daimon calld it "Melody"
and spoke, again, of our Author's delight
        in various Truth.

[Adam *steps forward and addresses the world in soliloquy, leaving* Eve *alone. As if he were her awareness that she has been left,* Samael *enters and hovers about* Eve, *unseen, but a presence felt, a voice heard.*]

Adam   O to keep the law of this Eden-side
             must be an easy thing!
                     to be true to a pure pleasure
             set beyond pain! for who would
             disobey the happiness of a song?

Samael   Eve!

Adam   I'll name all things anew for Eden's sake.
             Elm, thou art "Elm", Elk,
             thou art "Elk", Elder, thou art "Elder",
             and by your names grow in my heart to rime.

             See, how all the trees of the garden dance
             and beasts of the field keep company with Love
             when we but name them in time and tune
             as the high Romance of Eden bids us do.

Samael   Eve.

Eve   Who is there?

Adam   O Eve, we have a fellow in the Sun.
             How easy are the orders of this place!
             He lights up Day and I am Day.

	My brothers Wind and Cloud sail free and I sail free!
Samael	Samael.
Eve	What do you want?
Adam	My brother birds fly up and sing. The dancing grasses of the field below are answering. Come, Meadowlark! Come, Bobolink, Oriole, take wing, for in your fellow flight my heart takes wing.
Samael	Darkness, Eve. A moment of darkness, Eve. There is no darkness in your sight. I would undeceive you of this thing.
Eve	No! I heard you before. If all this bright ring, life's tree, deceives, it is a gay deceit.
Adam	O happy fear! God's magic art is rare. The orient tiger's power increases every joy. His stride, his glaring eye, his stripes of wrath and woe, in one great work combined, his natural robe, go as he goes, to teach us lordly measures in our song.
Samael	Question the song. Take thought of yesterday and tomorrow. This place knows nothing of them. There is no time here. If you had time, the world would be yours. God has removed you from your own ground into a silly magic of Eternity—it's but a word— in which you are nothing and you rejoice.

Adam	My heart leaps up in praise to see
	      how fierce and kind
	      this world abounds
	      in signs of animal majesty,
	and Adam and Eve like lions or tigers move
	in hidden measures of their love.

Samael	Are *you* Eve? He would see you now in the lion. See, Adam stands in a rapture of Eve over there, and you are here. He need not turn to you. Each leaf, each flower, each cunning beast—the tiger in his power, the lamb in his weakness—is Eve.
Eve	Adam! Adam!
Adam	O happy Eve. O fearful Eve. Abundance and fragrance of my world. Orchard of many trees, bid Spring once more amidst its watering springs bud forth.
Samael	Adam is seald in a promise you could break. For in this promise all the world is Woman. There is no division in his sight, God has so wedded each in each. Let me teach you the risk whereby the universe may be divided as it is. But break the bond, and you will be his woman, only you will be the gate calld Eve.
Eve	How could I know more of him? All Eden illustrates what he is to me.
Samael	But all things are not he. He is not all things. Love only *him* in him.
Eve	Only him? Only me? Will that be more?

Samael	Much more.

There is not only this tree of many trees,
there is an other tree of many trees
in which you will see thru the magic
of this tree where all things swim in a common life
and, having the knowledge of that tree,
  divide

light from light, sun from moon,
within from without, man from woman,
above from below, this side from that side,
good from evil, nation from nation—

  much more.

Let me tell you of the yearning that
  will come of it.
There will be news of Love.

Eve	But this is Love.

Samael	That will be Love.

Eve	How could I know?

Samael	I have come to show you. Let me kiss you with what I know.

Eve	Is it the Tree of Life?

Samael	It is the Tree of the Other Side, of what is more.

[Eve *closes her eyes, and* Samael *kisses her, awakening in her the grievous knowledge of the denial of love in which he dwells. A muted cry of anguish rises in* Eve.]

Eve	ohhhh. ohhhh.

Samael	In me the kiss is untrue. In me the tree is death. Now you have taken breath under a new law.

Go to Adam. He does not know.
Kiss him to make the kiss true.

Eve   My love for him lasts.

Samael   Yes, your love for him lasts.
             It's only a *passing* shame you feel.

Eve   Adam! Adam!

Adam   Yes?

Eve   O Adam, something has happend, I know!
             I am ashamed. O
             heal me with a kiss.

[*She kisses* Adam. *The stage is plunged into darkness.*]

Adam   The dark! The dark!

[*From off-stage we hear* Mrs Maybe's *voice as* Nature *entering with
her kerosene lamp.*]

Mrs Maybe   There, there. Never mind the dark.
             I'm coming with a little light.

THE END

CYPARISSUS

(From Ovid's *Metamorphoses* as translated by
Henry T. Riley for Bohn's Library in 1902)

Next the god sang of Cyparissus,
for there was among the many trees
drawn in the enchantment of Orpheus' song
a cypress that stood far off alone
at the end of a spine of trees
like the goal that stands in the Roman circus
at the end of the *spina* in the chariot race.

Now a tree, he was once a youth
beloved by Apollo whose strings
fit lyre and bow to a common music
so that the bent wood sings
and the man touching the divine instrument
touches upon the heart's
and upon the tree's sorrow in one melody,
finding that mode where love and death
move living things
as if they were expressions of one soul.

There was once a stag, a beast
sacred to the Nymphs of the Carthaean field,
splendid with antlers, king,
his head lovely in the shade of his branching crown,
his neck hung round with gleaming lights,

a bridal necklace such as women now wear
of gold, emeralds, amber, awakening
amorous wonder in men's eyes.

And, like a bride, he too
had put aside his natural fear,
so husbanded by love he knew
no rumor there of hurt or harm
but sought the loving hands of men
as they sought him
transformd by the charm of his lordly grace.

You, above all others, Cyparissus,
loved and sought him out. Among the youths
your beauty, most like his, shown bright.

You led him to lie down in new pastures
and to the springs of running waters.
You wreathed his antlers with various flowers
and, seated on his back like a horseman,
rode in one form, guiding his mouth
with the bridle of your love his love obeyd.

It was Summer. In the mid-day heat
the stag, fatigued,
laid his body down on the grassy bank,
resting in the dappled shade of a tree.

How did you wound him? It is
as if man had great need of some agony,
for the youth Cyparissus,
knowing, yet unknowing,
pierced the lordly heart with his spear
and drew the life blood from his side,
so that now as the god Orpheus sings
his song remembers the grief of that wound.

I too, drawing the story again from Ovid's pen,
know the bewildering knowledge in the beast's gaze
that searcht with trust his lover's eyes
and found his own wound repeated there.
For love binds heart to human heart
and would sound the depth
from which the mortal life cries out. Apollo's art
that from the lyre
sends notes to pierce the human soul
from which the life of music flows
sends the arrow from the bow.

Apollo! Cyparissus cried: O Phoebus!
Upon the strings of your terror my hand has strayd
and struck to wound so that my lover died.
And I would die, but I cannot die.

As if to console, the god replied,
speaking in the wisdom of immortal mind,
ignorant of care, words without cure.
For what did Apollo know before Hyacinth
that all men know of death and loss?

But moved by the beauty of Cyparissus
he removed him into the beauty of a pure lament.
He bent grief, as he bends Love ever,
into an immortal fever without relief.
So that Cyparissus begd of our Father Zeus
some lonely change in what he was
that he might mourn, some form
to emerge from his inconsolate weeping
—his hair stiffening into black leaves,
his body flung out against the sky
as if speaking forever
man's stark cry remembering death.

Then Apollo filld therefrom
the need for sorrow the Sun has.
For the deep of the god's light
is a cup that needs man's weeping to be filld
and He brings ever
changes of joy and grief therefore, like Orpheus,
deriving his art from what men suffer,
and would strike at the heart
to make his song.

Thou shalt ever,
Cyparissus, be mournd as you mourn,
and no man sorrowing for the dead
will be alone but in this tree Cypress
        have his friend.

A PART-SEQUENCE FOR CHANGE

1

If they had cursed the man,
dried back the water in the spring
by boiling water in a frying pan
until the thirsty sun
feard for the songs that he once sang
and burnd to sing,

over *them* the cursed image
over *them* the blackend thing.

2

I shall draw back
and among my sacred objects

gather the animal power back,
the force that in solitude
works in me its leases,
the night-bird's voice
in the day's verses.

The flame in the body of the lamp
fumes upon the surface of the glass.
The boy I was watches
not without fear
black places in the darkening room
where animal faces
appear and pass away

and reappear.

3

Estranged. Deeply estranged.
Fish caught in no net,
hand at the harp without strings
striking the dark air for music,
having no more than the need
to go by.

Deeply estranged.
For I have been let go from what
I felt in the music.
I have been deserted by the words spoken
in the rapture of being deserted,

of the rising meshes, the escaping waters,
                    the writhing and
therein thriving catch of fishes
raised by the Fisher out of my solitude
into the acclaiming throng without me.

But say they take this song up
and in the threads of their voices
these words appear (mine) (theirs).
Estranged. Deeply estranged.

Once more the young days of the year
find out the invisible ranges
and break from the tree
changes and turnings of the heart,
the swarm of too many buds
for melody

and the ascendancy of the shadow
in the blossoming mass.

STRUCTURE OF RIME XIX

(for Shirley and Wally Berman)

The artists of the survival wet the animal stones to reflect their faces. Eyes in the pavement return to the street lights rimes and rings ensouling the way we go. Under the branches of tears, the falling crowns of night's dew.

At the turn of the path where it is steep we saw Jupiter climbing ahead of us and turnd his image in the hand mirror. As a lone brilliant in the thick of eyelashes. As a star in the stare under the closed lids. As the far sun's light caught in the lantern of Jupiter to the mind's reflection.

How to shape survival! In what art to survive! The alchemist draws gold into gold. The money changers set up their tables at the edges of the park where our dreams go. The grass momentarily gold in reflections cast by our search lights, the trees shedding gold, and willfully the artists of the survival lose their last coins among the waves and shadows of their work.

Now I have nothing left and will not survive. Freed from the promises of what I was, my old longing rises, a raised cup from a hand that trembles, where sight itself is a brim of water surrounded by waters of what it does not see.

STRUCTURE OF RIME XX

The Master of Rime told me, You must learn to lose heart. I have darkend this way and you yourself have darkend. Are you so blind you cant see what you cant see?

You keep the unknown bird hidden in your hands as if to carry sight into the house. But the sightless ones have opend the windows and listen to the songs outside. *Absence,* the Mother of this Blindness tells them, *rimes among the feathers of birds that exist only in sight. The songs you hear fall from their flight light like shadows stars cast among you.*

You must learn to lose your heart. Let the beat of your heart go. Missing the beat. And from the care of your folded hands unfold a feeling in the room of an empty space. For the pit of despair wants you to come there. The thrush waits trembling in the confinement of his master's doubt and every bird among the watery eaves sings as his brother.

O brother of the confined! O my twin lord of the net rime has tied in the tongues of fire.

And the Master of Rime appeard again, smiling. His hands cupt as he went. His head bowd, looking down, seeking his way away from me.

STRUCTURE OF RIME XXI

(for Louise & George Herms)

Lost in the hour-maze of our Father, Time. He came in time!

For his solitude he made a herm of wood. Sending roads out from the heart of the wood to the dry meadows beyond. Cloud fragments torn loose from the solid sheen of the moon.

The electric lamp in the isinglass casing. The painted shadow on the glare of the plate. The like lightness of the plate when lifted. All these things left in the design of the maze.

Slowly the ear turns in time round to the sound it is listening for. The coil of thickness let fall from the table. But here there is no floor to the melody. In the broken plate arcs of higher sympathies cross actual tones and erect in the lonely herm the musician sees a window.

So that the dark itself persists in the window like a lamp I said. A depresst key that sounds in the piano. And the sun returning to day returns in the old way he has always returnd.

The women following the sun release the sound from steps of the wood. Bird-notes of a ladder at the edge of the silence.

THE CONTINENT

Under-
earth currents, Gaia, Hannahanna,
mother of the Lady Verdure
all dresst in green
her leafy graces, in margins

the writ illumined, wreathed round
with pomegranate
split for in-betweens of jeweld hive
red seed upon red seed,
ripe peach, pear, apple cut
to show the core,

vine tendril into talon curls,
faces in the fruit occur.
The artist of the margin
works abundancies

and sees the theme is much too big
to cover all o'er, a decorative frieze
out of earthly proportion to the page,

needs vast terms, unspecified
even boredom of those
plains that from Denver bend
east, east, east.

The mid-Western mind
differs in essentials
—another time zone.
In Iowa they do not dig

172

the swarming locale, this port of
recall. There's no
Buddhist temple in the mid-West town.

Earth drains down the Old Man River and runs out
in swamps and shallows of the Caribbean.

They do not remember the body of
   them waters
but stand with feet upon the ground
   against the
run to the mythic sea, the fabulous.

       II

             A diary poem
to Day, Gaia, Earth
—murther, murmurer, demurrer.

The old have crept out to day
after noon and go out so slow
forth lifting up their bones
painfully—it's a caution
 to see their faring.   Then

a sparrow smasht upon the sidewalk.

I'm not so old but I can put
the thought away, my foot
before my foot,
climbing the hill as if for rime
my teeth are gnashing, and again
the thought returns
that we conquer life itself to live,
survive what we are.

III

The head crusht sideways, the wings
                   spread out
as if embracing the sidewalk, too close
                   for shadow,
the immediate!   How bright the sun
                   surrounds them,
and day by day they
                   sun themselves

                   turning

a day's eye turning as the sun passes
over head.

IV

These figures: a snake-coil of water,
       a bird-wheel in the sky,
to the great wheel of sooty shear-waters
       passing north
counter-clockwise as far as the
       horizon
between shore and the islands

make their announcement
in the heart of things. Here
our West's the Orient,
our continent the sea.

In the heart itself a pang
as if the very Day moved northward
over the face of the waters.

The mass of clouds moves up against
    the voice, bright breasts
blinding the eye as I attack
    their moving front to find
a place in which the eye might rest.

                    v

I am so far from you,
come up the years
so far, a continent
looms between.

In the far, the Appalachians
belong to time before our time
the Urals are a part of.

Continents of water and of earth,
Gaia! Time's mother too
must wear guises,
hop on one leg
and hide her head in a hut,
dance with the rest among the maskt guys.

It's still Saturday
before Easter
and Love's hero lies
in the nest of our time.

In Banyalbufar the little doll of the Virgin
once more meets the sorrowing procession,
the black-clad walkers
before the green of April, and looks upon
His corpse they carry forth
to meet her.

Effeminized, the soul is Sleeping Beauty
or Snow White who waits
for Sunday's kiss to wake her.
Time zone by time zone

across the continent dawn so comes
breaking the shell of flowers
a wave
Earth makes in turning
a crest
against tomorrow breaks.

VI

There is only the one time.
There is only the one god.
There's only the one promise

and from its flame
the margins of the page flare forth.
There's only the one page,

the rest remains
in ashes. There is only
the one continent, the one sea—

moving in rifts, churning, enjambing,
drifting feature from feature.

New Directions Paperbooks—A Partial Listing

For complete listing request free catalog from
New Directions, 80 Eighth Avenue, New York 10011   †Bilingual

For complete listing request free catalog from
New Directions, 80 Eighth Avenue, New York 10011   †**Bilingual**